THE REALITY OVERLOAD

THE REALITY OVERLOAD

The Modern World's Assault on the Imaginal Realm

ANNIE LE BRUN

Translated by Jon E. Graham

Inner Traditions
Rochester, Vermont

Inner Traditions
One Park Street
Rochester, Vermont 05767
www.InnerTraditions.com

Originally published in French under the title *Du trop de réalité* by Éditions Stock, 31, rue de Fleurus — 75006 Paris
First U.S. edition published in 2008 by Inner Traditions

Library of Congress Cataloging-in-Publication Data

Le Brun, Annie.
[Du trop de réalité. English]
The reality overload : the modern world's assault on the imaginal realm / Annie Le Brun ; translated by Jon E. Graham. — 1st U.S. ed.
p. cm.
"Originally published in French under the title Du trop de réalité by Éditions Stock"—T.p. verso.
Includes bibliographical references and index.
ISBN 978-1-59477-244-3
1. Civilization, Modern—1950– 2. Postmodernism—Social aspects. I. Graham, Jon. II. Title.
CB428.L3813 2008
909.82—dc22

2008034241

Printed and bound in the United States by Lake Book Manufacturing

10 9 8 7 6 5 4 3 2 1

Text design by Diana April and layout by Priscilla Baker
This book was typeset in Garamond Premier Pro with Versailles used as a display typeface

CONTENTS

TRANSLATOR'S FOREWORD

ANNIE LE BRUN, ECOLOGIST OF THE IMAGINAL REALM

The poet is the guilty conscience of the world.

PIERRE-JEAN JOUVE

The work of Annie Le Brun, only a small portion of which has been translated into English, truly stands alone. As a surrealist poet, her writing is that of a communicating vessel in which the poetic and the critical, the sensorial and the intellectual are constantly shaping and reinvesting themselves in each other. The heightened intricacies and layers of meaning this creates allows her to neatly sidestep the common ideological and theoretical constructs that now claim the cultural landscape as their domain and restore to the creative act of communication transformational—or what could also be called magical—power. Though she disdains the label of writer as a profession, Le Brun has produced a brilliant body of work, whose sophistication and subtlety resist superficial reading and offer unique and unparalleled insights for those who join her on her poetic soundings of the contemporary landscape. Stamford professor and author Jean-Marie Apostolides notes: "To read Annie Le Brun is to go beyond conventional signification: it is to accept an unusual thought, which seeks its expression in poetical language: it is to abandon oneself to a sensibility, which permits an intellectual drift outside the common path."

Born in Rennes, France, in 1942, Annie Le Brun resolved at an early age to abandon the well-trodden paths offered her by society and to carve her own way. (She notes that Rennes offered the best fare to nourish revolt, being the city where Alfred Jarry created Ubu.) Her trajectory intersected with that of André Breton, the Czech painter Toyen, and other surrealists (including her companion Radovan Ivsic). When she was still in her early twenties, she became an active participant in surrealist group activities, including the final exhibition to be mounted before the death of Breton, *L'Écart absolu* [Absolute Divergence], a fierce and humorous assault on consumer society. Unbowed by the disarray that overtook the surrealists following Breton's death, she continued her life journey by writing only what she felt compelled to write, rejecting all the honorifics, grants, and compensations that society offers artists that relegate them to the status of indentured servants and specialists in subversion. She turned down the prestigious literary prize offered one of her books by the Académie Française, with no public fanfare or posturing. Another attempt by a former minister of culture to award her a medal of national merit was rejected just as quietly and unhesitatingly.

Her writing includes poems; groundbreaking works on the Gothic novel, Sade, and Roussel; as well as a trenchant critique of modern neofeminism that earned her the charge of being a traitor to her sex. But she rigorously avoids the black-and-white dichotomies that animate most criticisms, as her attacks on neofeminism offer no consolation to male chauvinists. And as readers will see in *The Reality Overload,* Le Brun targets equally both the promoters of postmodernism and the advocates of a return to the Western canon who attempt to channel into a stagnant current the very murmur of life that dares to threaten the construction of their ideological citadels.

> The European artist in the twentieth century can counter the desiccation of his wellspring of inspiration, which rationalism and utilitarianism have brought about, only by reviving the so-called primitive vision, a synthesis of sensorial representation and mental representation.
>
> ANDRÉ BRETON

A key concern of Annie Le Brun is imagination. For her, the assault by the modern world on dream and imagination is a calamity that—while seemingly minor in appearance—is, in fact, the greatest problem of all because it makes possible all the other devastations threatening our world today. Le Brun is also concerned about Eros and individual revolt. If these cannot be restored their sovereignty, then all our efforts to solve the problems facing us are doomed to failure. These leitmotifs run through all of Annie Le Brun's work and were key to the surrealist project and its goal to reenvision humankind in its entirety.

Surrealism—which was bedeviled since day one by legions of critics, shovels in hand, eager to dig its grave—is singularly misunderstood today. The birth of surrealism has generally been ascribed to the revolt of a younger generation against a civilization that created the carnage of the First World War, all the while citing the pretexts of reason and morality. The surrealist movement was, in fact, a revolutionary attempt to keep alive the magic ideology that was the hallmark of the thinking of primitive man and medieval magi within the concept of a radically new environment—the urban landscape created by the industrial revolution. The first to grasp this new human landscape and inaugurate a poetry that could apprehend it was Baudelaire.* The occult concerns of many of the poets who followed him, such as Nerval, Hugo, and Rimbaud, figured prominently in their creative output. Poets of this stripe, like the surrealists who picked up their cause, were not seeking simply to create poems but to capture the awareness that goes into the creative process and infuse it into the very fabric of everyday life. Like alchemy, the main purpose of their writing was to inspire altered states of consciousness capable of perceiving the point where, as stated in the Second Manifesto of Surrealism, opposites cease to be contradictory. For these writers, poetry is a vehicle of higher consciousness that stands apart from the awareness described by orthodox religious thinking. This is key

*Baudelaire was the first modern poet to grapple with the new human fauna created by the industrial revolution, such as the flâneur (idler) and the ragpicker (the creation of mass production gave new value to garbage), a notion explored in great depth by the German author and critic Walter Benjamin in his essays on Baudelaire.

to what Baudelaire called the most scientific of faculties: the imagination, "because it alone understands the universal analogy or what mystical religion calls correspondence."*

Many of the common surrealist techniques for achieving this charged poetic consciousness are well known: exquisite corpses, the manufacture of oneiric and poetic objects, and techniques borrowed from classic spiritualism such as automatic writing and trance states. However, there is also a persistent attempt to reenergize the poetic charges that lie latent in everyday life, defused into commonplace expressions. Like Breton, who was especially gifted at this kind of repoeticization, Le Brun is constantly redeploying commonplace terms in unusual juxtapositions and combinations so that the only way to truly comprehend her meaning is to take the words completely literally. Two immediate examples are furnished by the titles of two earlier Le Brun essays, *Appel d'air* and *Qui Vive. Appel d'air* is French for air intake but translates literally as "A Plea for Air." *Qui Vive* is the automatic command of sentries demanding: Who goes there? Literally, it means "Who is alive" or "Who's living?" Similarly, Breton's collection of essays *Les Pas Perdus* would translate in accordance with conventional French usage as "The Waiting Rooms" but done literally would be "The Lost Steps." The purpose of this technique, according to Breton, is to restore a more decisive role to words. He goes on to say, "Nothing is gained by modifying them since, just as they are, they respond so promptly to our call." He ends this paragraph (which appears in his essay *Introduction au discours dur le peu de réalité* [Introduction to the discourse on the reality scarcity]) asking: Doesn't the mediocrity of our universe stem essentially from our powers of enunciation?"

One important way to view *The Reality Overload* is as a photographic negative of the reality scarcity Breton discusses in his "Introduction"

*André Breton mentioned in an interview "the idea of a 'hieroglyphic' key to the world. It more or less existed before all high poetry, which can only be moved by the principles of analogies and correspondences. Poets such as Hugo, Nerval, Baudelaire, and Rimbaud, or thinkers such as Fourier, share this idea with the occultists and likely also with the rigor of scientific inventors." A more recent text by the poet and playwright Radovan Isvic describes the current crisis of the world as a crisis in magic.

essay. In appropriate fashion, Breton introduces a discourse that was never written, therefore providing a perfect illustration of just what he meant by a paucity of reality. Where Breton's text reveals the essentially finite properties of reality and how to go beyond it, in *The Reality Overload* Annie Le Brun has chosen to confront the invasive power of a willfully more finite concept of reality, one that uses verbosity and oxymoron to cement its dominance.

Peppering *The Reality Overload* are phrases that function like *anti*-advertising slogans. These phrases reveal the various strategies that make our cultural and environmental terrains hostile to anything that would obstruct or curtail their current functioning. One of the primary weapons in this process is what Le Brun calls the rationality of inconsistency, which is used to create severe cognitive dissonance in our minds. Other unique Le Brun phrases include corporeal illiteracy, concrete dematerialization, reciprocal neutralization, and lateral critique. While many of the examples she offers to illustrate these phrases are originally French, astute readers will be able to find no shortage of these types of discordant examples in the United States. As one example, "lateral critique" refers to the numerous discussions found in academic and political arenas that provide only sideways commentaries. They never get to the bottom of the topic at hand. Opposing viewpoints offered merely for their "reciprocal neutralization" are painfully visible in the canned television debate shows providing political analyses before and after every announcement, decision, or event. When Jon Stewart, the host of Comedy Central's *The Daily Show,* appeared on the program *Crossfire,* he wasted no time scolding the two hosts for their "partisan hackery" and asked them to stop hurting the country with their charade. While *Crossfire* never recovered from this criticism and was pulled from the air, other shows continue to offer the political equivalent of staged wrestling matches.

More important is Le Brun's rejection of the rationalist model in favor of an analogical one. Even modernism's most acute critics of the ravages caused by unchecked rationalism were incapable of formulating their critiques without resorting to reason. By operating within the rationalist confines, these critics removed whatever transformational power their arguments might otherwise have had. Le Brun turns rather to Novalis and his "true historical sense, the prophetically visionary sense that finds its explanation based on the profound and infinite correlation that connects the entire world." Analogy can connect body and mind, objective space and subjective space, and the animal, plant, and mineral realms in a way that logic cannot. It is the key to the groundbreaking correlations Le Brun makes between the environmental degradation of our physical world and the ravages suffered by the imaginal realm of our minds. The relationship between the disappearance of the great mammals like the blue whale and the great rebels of times past is the same insidious and pervasive decay as the depreciation and adulteration of language and the genetic modification of the foods we eat. In all the cases she cites, it is clear that the shackles placed on human imagination have made possible the environmental and social degradation that pervades our modern world. For Annie Le Brun, the most horrendous ecological catastrophe is found in "the growing impossibility to imagine the symbolic exchange that never stops occurring between ideas, beings, and things."*

The fierceness of Le Brun's criticism stems from the fact that there are many who are actively seeking to stop environmental stewardship in the interests of the mercantile relationships that are the core of the modern world. As the French philosopher Dany-Robert Dufour says in his book *The Art of Shrinking Heads,* "What neoliberalism wants is a desymbolized subject who is neither subject to guilt nor able to rely on a critical free will." The reality overload is, as if by design, best at creating the kind of sensorial climate control in which all critical mean-

*On its publication, *Du trop de réalité* received a good deal of attention from the Green community of France, and the author was interviewed in the environmentalist press and appeared at seminars such as the one sponsored by the *Écologiste* on the dangers of genetically modified organisms (GMOs). This may have been the first time that such a conference featured a speaker who opened her remarks with a quote from Sade: "All intellectual ideas are so greatly subordinate to Nature's physical aspect that the comparisons supplied us by agriculture will never morally lead us astray."

ing is diluted, discouraged, and eliminated. As Annie Le Brun shows, there are multiple enterprises at work to replace the imaginary with the virtual, which smothers the subversive poetic charge—a charge that has been a core feature of the great works of art, literature, and philosophy produced over the centuries. Just as an environment constantly filled with noise creates dysfunctional reactions in people and animals, the overabundance of lateral critique by the academic community and established "experts" in these fields makes it impossible for the poetic charge of these works to function properly. The very analysis and excessive commentary on what the work is in effect buries the work and makes it impossible to see what it actually is.

But Le Brun takes pains to point out that this information overload does not, in fact, lead to an overwhelming amount of choices, as some analysts have suggested. Rather, she says, it is "the impossibility of being put back within a consistent, tangible arrangement that makes any one piece of information—whether worthless or important—seem condemned to being lost in the flow of all the rest. What's more, the uninterrupted procession of this information shuts down every perspective, one by one—perspectives that until now were the natural sites in which the imagination could project itself past simple data in order to grasp a being, an event, or a situation."

Shortly after the initial release of *Du trop de réalité* in 2000, the French daily *Le Monde* ran an article about Annie Le Brun in which she said: "I have been finding living more and more difficult for the last few years. The spirit of the times has become intolerable to me. Is it only because I'm getting older? But I am not the only person feeling this way. The critical weapons (Marxism, Situationism) we once had at our disposal no longer can explain the current discontent in our civilization. There are extremely interesting, meticulous criticisms on the new National Library [of France], mad cow disease [etc.] that are right on target, but the connection between all of them is never shown. There is a worldwide effort underfoot to model sensibility. The devastation of the Brazilian and German forests has its equivalent in the cultural domain.

If we have good reason to be alarmed by adulterated food, we have just as much reason to distrust the cultural nourishment we are being served—which is worth no more than imitation crab. The power grab in the sensory cultural domain is accompanied by a gradually increasing insensitivity, to the detriment of our relationship to beings and things. We are experiencing a dematerialization of our relationship with the world, which some are striving to replace with a fictitious materiality."

Against the willfully incoherent landscape created by the reality overload, Annie Le Brun raises the call for a passion-based existence that allows us to see and experience the natural interdependency of individuals and things, of the human being and the environment. So much has been put into play to make us forget the kind of existence offered by passion, which both unites us with the world and differentiates us from it completely. The first step we must take to reclaim our relationship to the world, our imagination, and our dreams is to say no, no, a thousand times no. Fortunately, as Le Brun reminds us, while servitude is contagious, freedom is even more so.

JON E. GRAHAM
JUNE 2008

Jon E. Graham has translated more than thirty books from the French, including the award-winning *Books on Fire* by Lucien Polastron, *The Secret Message of Jules Verne* by Michel Lamy, and *Immaculate Conception* by André Breton and Paul Eluard. Mr. Graham's translation of Jean-Luc Steinmetz's *Arthur Rimbaud: Presence of an Enigma* was selected by the *Los Angeles Times* as one of the ten best translations of 2000. As a graphic artist, his works have been displayed in galleries in New York, Philadelphia, San Diego, Seattle, Vancouver, Paris, Prague, Stockholm, and the National Art Museum of Portugal in Lisbon. His illustrations have appeared in various books and magazines. He is the acquisitions editor for Inner Traditions International, a position he has held since 1996.

PREFACE

There are some books that a person would rather not write. But the abject nature of our time is such that I feel obliged to break my silence, especially when such great efforts are being made to convince us that no revolt is taking place. On this point as on many others, I find it repugnant to put faith in the word of a faithless society that finds its preferred mode of expression in denial.

In the natural rhythm of the returning seasons, children slip between their dreams each morning, still able to fold like a handkerchief the reality awaiting them. The very sky reflected in a mud puddle is close enough for them to touch. So why are there no longer any adolescents wild enough to instinctively refuse the sinister future that is being prepared for them? Why are there no longer any young people impassioned enough to stray beyond the restricted vistas that they are taught to mistake for life? Why are there no longer any individuals determined enough to oppose by all possible means the system of cretinization from which our era draws its consensual strength? Such questions as these provide me sufficient reason to speak out, even when so many things dissuade me from doing so.

Priding myself on not occupying any easily locatable position on the desolate horizon that people shamelessly call the "intellectual landscape," I know I have little chance of being heard, and even less likelihood of being understood. Furthermore, my natural repulsion for any kind of affiliation keeps me at a distance from the countless pressure groups that our era urges everyone to join. It seems that the single great requirement of life today is that we indiscriminately identify ourselves as something—as a woman, a Breton,* a sportsman, or even a pedophile—just as long as we renounce all claim to being an individual.

But I have neither self-interest nor party to defend. I do not have the slightest concern about protecting my intellectual authority, something I have never even wished to possess. I have never been in any real danger of falling into this trap, because I have been truly impressed only by the magnificent invention of a revolt waged by a few select individuals against "the unacceptable human condition." These individuals have always been too dedicated to their dreams to waste any effort trying to play a role in the world, unless doing so would completely change the cards dealt here. To my eyes, though, their intractable refusal—conscious or not—to stick to the status quo is the only thing that can still give meaning to an existence apparently condemned to having less and less.

But now we see that such paths, ignored until recent years precisely because of the extent to which they deviate, have come to be regarded gradually as historical, literary, or artistic curiosities. The countless flunkies who increasingly clutter universities and museums can take pride in this result. Evidently, the essential purpose behind the feverish activity of these diploma-holding road crews is to clear our cultural highways, tossing to the shoulder all ways of thinking that carry within them any promise of different ways of living.

Far from being an epiphenomenon of the history of these last few years, I see this situation as something quite the opposite: the effect of an operation of standardization that insidiously renders us more powerless by disarming us to an unprecedented extent. In this way, nothing less than the buried treasure of all future freedom is devalued (rather than being within reach of all of us, as we are led to believe), solely through

*[The Bretons—the people of Brittany, in western France—form a distinct ethnic group, with their own language and culture. —*Ed.*]

open exploitation at the hands of deductive reasoning. Systematically torn from the night of their profound coherence, these treasures are reduced to signs that eventually drift far from meaning. As catastrophe follows catastrophe, we may well wonder if the resulting proliferation of insignificance is even more alarming than the disappearance of the ozone layer. Have we forgotten that imaginary objects are just as necessary for our survival?

As Paul Valéry* observed at the end of the World War I, "We other civilizations now know that we are mortal." Then he adds, "All is not lost, but everything feels as though it is dying . . ." He still placed faith in a jump start of the mind, even if it took the worst kind of crisis to trigger it.

Unfortunately, we can no longer even nurture hopes of such a jump start today; now everything is hastening to its ruin, while business goes on as usual, as if nothing seems to be dying. Further, while various critical positions have emerged recently to denounce such and such a dysfunction, none of these criticisms has been able to take the true measure of the tangible devastation that accompanies such a widespread blindness. Pertinent though many of these analyses may be, they are all lacking the "true historical sense" that Novalis spoke of, the "prophetically visionary sense that finds its explanation based on the profound and infinite correlation that connects the entire world."†

There have been previous attempts to create an inclusive critique, but these endeavors have been limited to using the tools provided by reason—which makes it only sadder to see that, despite their intention

*[Paul Valéry (1871–1945) was a French poet, essayist, and philosopher. He was a member of the Académie Française (French Academy) and was considered to be the last of the French Symbolists. —*Ed.*]

†["Echt historischer Sinn ist der prophetische Visionssinn-erklärbar aus dem tiefen unendlichen Zusammenhange der ganzen Welt." From Novalis (Georg Philipp Friedrich Leopold, Freiherr von Hardenberg, 1772–1801), *Werke und Briefe* (Leipzig: Insel-Verlag, 1942), 417 (Fragment 2358). —*Ed.*]

to combat the state of things more effectively, the authors of such critiques have nothing to offer that is capable of opposing a movement of devastation in which all is interconnected not logically but *analogically.* To remain ignorant of this constitutes a serious threat to what very little freedom we still possess.

PART ONE

I

THE NETWORK PRISON

More than seventy years ago, a surrealist flier exhorted, "You who do not see think of those who see!" It was a flier that would soon grow heavier with a premonitory weight. In fact, it has been a long time since the senses first perceived a crime perpetrated against life, but because the essential characteristic of this crime has been to cause a progressive anesthesia, only a rare few have followed the full scope of its developments. What I depicted in *Appel d'air* [Air Intake] in 1988, then in *Qui vive* [Who Goes There] in 1991, has been only confirmed since then: We can no longer doubt the existence of a phenomenon that the vast majority seems hardly capable of perceiving—worse, there are those who strive to muddy the waters even more.

I will not go back over the origin of this state of affairs. I have attributed it to the threat of nuclear destruction, which—solely by virtue of having rendered our general annihilation possible—has paralyzed our power of resistance, while at the same time enclosing us all the more easily in a reality that holds us hostage. I have also discussed poetic violence as it has emerged continually from certain gestures, encounters, and currents of thought (although certainly not from what is produced today under the pretext of poetry, which is nothing but a pretentious embellishment of boredom). I showed how this unpredictable violence, with its age-old light, could still illuminate all that we are taught to forget once and for all.

It was not a shot in the dark, but a certainty: Without this light, improbable though it may sound, we are incapable of knowing what weapons we still have at our disposal. Yet after less than ten years, the most alarming prospects envisioned nearly a decade ago had come true. Should we see this as cause and effect, with the simultaneous emergence of what is now called the "networked society"?[1] Does this go hand in hand with a world increasingly dominated by computerized communication?

Undoubtedly, it is not that simple, even though the advent of these new modes of exchange accommodates, if not encourages, ideas and lifestyles that seem to have an entirely new origin. Nevertheless, there are historical coincidences that invite us to wonder, for example, if there is a relationship among the crisis in poetry, the collapse of certain ecological niches, the rise of religious fundamentalism, and soil desertification. It is completely possible that this sort of question, incongruous though it may have been even in the recent past, may now be answered by certain behaviors or opinions encouraged or even engendered by this "networked society." It is as if a completely different reality has begun to manifest through these networks, without anyone even perceiving how strange this reality is.

In this reality, the labyrinth of circuits is far stronger than the walls against which some of us bang our heads. We can recall René Crevel:* "You swine! We know your schools, your colleges, your places of pleasure and suffering. If they inspire us at all, it is to smash our faces against your mosaics of filthy little self-interests, which serve as the floors, walls, and ceilings of your public buildings and private dwellings."

Now, the difference is that while these same "filthy little self-interests" are far from disappearing, it is impossible to see beyond the horizon of their mosaics of spite, meanness, and shamelessness. They circulate, meet, and propagate in a flood in which user-friendliness

*[René Crevel (1900–1935) was a French surrealist writer. —*Ed.*]

competes with tolerance. We find ourselves facing a reality that rejects nothing and nobody—a reality that never stops trying to head us off—and because it is in constant motion, it has become completely invasive. It is a disproportionate reality in which the overabundance, accumulation, and saturation of information force events into the collision of an excess of time and an excess of space.

But, as some so ardently strive to make us believe, even as it launches ambush after ambush upon the unreality of our desires, there is nothing "virtual" about this reality. In fact, it is overflowing, a *reality overload,* coming to besiege us at the very depths of our being.

Even if an almost universal inability to connect events, ideas, and forms to the bodies that produce them has remained the essential characteristic of the transition from one century to the next, the origin of this inability cannot be sought in the insurmountable difficulties inherent in grasping an elusive reality. Quite the contrary: This origin should be sought in the fact that it has become increasingly difficult to keep our distance from the status quo, if only so that we can discern what landscape is in the process of emerging—unbeknownst to us.

2

THE DEVALUATION OF DREAM

Is it because of its inordinate self-complacency that this era has not been able to stop marveling at the calamities it has spawned? Whether a defect of vision or an error of taste, the fact remains that none of us can contest that the twentieth century has won the grand prize for horrors. The only question is who can draw up the most complete list of these horrors and paint the most gripping picture of them? How can we deplore this, even if such analyses often arrive a bit late? Although others have described these horrors without appearing to notice, however, that fascinated by the wealth of the kaleidoscope offered to us and staggered by the excess of reality shown to us—we are no longer in any condition to determine which perspectives are vanishing or perceive which hues are disappearing.

What triumphs is an exterior darkness, resembling, if I may put it this way, a coat of exterior paint. The social, historical, and political darkness belonging to this category appears exclusively in the sorry images of the century just passed, and is now available to us only through memory. But what is remarkable is that the darkness dwelling within us has disappeared from the palette. It is as if we have forgotten who we are and the inner shadows we cast are not at all foreign to the misfortunes we encounter.

This is how the dream has vanished from our horizon. Is this state of affairs the result of the human sciences becoming respectable and of our acknowledgment of psychoanalysis? Whatever the correct answer, this disappearance of dream is one of the greatest deficiencies of the end of the millennium—and, to my eyes, falls just short of catastrophic.

No doubt, when we contemplate all the calamities that the twentieth century so generously supplied, stumbling upon a particular tragedy such as this disappearance of the dream would, by comparison, appear far smaller in scale—if it was not a disaster that could create many far greater ones. Indeed, this calamity is an amputation that strips us of everything we might have used to blindly rediscover the world from the most remote reaches of our solitude. Evidence for this resides in the fact that at the onset of the present era, no one has expressed anxiety at the disappearance of the "definitive dreamer"* who we may not yet have ceased to be. It even seems that in this disappearance some find a cause for rejoicing, for perhaps some have been working—consciously or otherwise—to bring about this catastrophe.

Now, however, is no longer the time to seek out the causes of this inner disaster that leads us to deceive ourselves about both who we are and who we could be. Rather, it is a good time to recall what Victor Hugo wrote in 1863: "We should create our life as one creates a dream." These words are from an essay inspired by his discovery thirty years earlier, aided by Arago's† telescope, of a mountain on the moon called the Promontory of Dream. Here Hugo, using the telescope of time, depicts an overwhelming spectacle of the dream as it is torn from its surrounding shadows. Using one of his habitual shifts to overturn what other men think, he connects the emergence of the dream to that of light: "There is no more mysterious sight than this irruption of the dawn into a universe covered in darkness. It is the right to life declaring itself in sublime proportions. It is the process of awakening given enormous

*["Definitive dreamer" is André Breton's definition of man in the *First Surrealist Manifesto*. —*Trans.*]

†[François Arago (1786–1853), French astronomer. —*Ed.*]

dimensions. It seems as if we are witnessing the payment of a debt to the infinite."

Through its height, this Promontory of Dream naturally reveals to us "the world that is not and that is." Victor Hugo requires nothing more to transform dream itself into a promontory towering over the abyss, a splendid concretion of what sometimes makes man much more than just himself.

In fact, everything that the end of the twentieth century has denied, hidden, or opposed is evoked here in all its violence, luxuriance, and innocence.

We can begin with the *infinite,* a word that has even become indecent to mention because of its dangers, which are so often depicted by petit bourgeois philosophy—all the better to lead us back into the cage of the finite. Yet it is this infinite, used as measurement and as perspective, that Victor Hugo shows us is within dream's reach—in order to convince each of us to rediscover it inside ourselves.

Hugo's declaration that "[n]o, no one is beyond dream; hence its immensity" is all we need in order to take the measure of the final years of a century that has worked overtime to condemn this fact to complete oblivion. Hence, the extremely limited scope of a school of criticism, which, with its mistrust of any imaginary perspective, has helped to narrow our horizons considerably, if unintentionally.

As Hugo insists, "[A]bandoning the surface, whether to climb or to descend, is always an adventure." He remains convinced that "every man is the adventurer of his own idea" and that "men always wish to dwell in this palace of the impossible," for the imprescriptible reason that "we live on questions asked of the imaginary world."

Because we must "leave the real" in order to "enter into the true," all that matters is the height of the viewpoint, which is directly proportional to the depth of the dive.

As Victor Hugo explains, we can be assured that "[t]hese encroachments on the shadow are not without danger. Dreaming has its casualties:

madmen. Here and there, in its dark corners, we meet cadavers of intelligence such as Tasso, Pascal, and Swedenborg. These delvers into the human soul are like highly exposed miners." But fear not! The onset of this new millennium has succeeded in replacing this adventurous verticality and all the risks of the freedom it brings with the endless horizontality of a shadow-free landscape.

This horizontality is confirmed and reinforced every day by a communications "network" that spells out a reality so full of itself that it ceaselessly outstrips itself in "virtual reality." It is the reality overload that engenders this virtual reality, which intends to encompass all reality insofar as "this is a system in which reality itself (that is to say the material/symbolic existence of people) is entirely captured and ensnared in a framework of virtual images, a universe of semblances, in which appearances are not only located on the screen—where the experience is communicated—but also have become the experience itself."[1]

Under these conditions, there is no longer any need for a higher viewpoint, and who today takes time to worry about something that does not exist? If everything henceforth is supposedly going to become real, then semblance already *is* reality in gestation. Or, at least, this is what we hear from experts who avoid the mistake of explaining that as a result, we are being told to evolve less in "virtual reality" and more in "real virtuality."[2]

To me, this does not constitute the kind of progress that inspires rejoicing, but instead explains why, in the last decade, the dream and subsequently the imagination as a dream of the body, along with the body as the shadow of the imaginary realm, have simply become obsolete. That there is never any mention of this is proof not that the phenomenon does not exist, but rather that it existed as a reality before it was murdered.

If, up to now, technical criticism has not offered words on this point, the recent infatuation for Situationist theses,* which are even

*[The Situationist movement, in Paris, originated in the early 1950s. It was created by a group of avant-garde intellectuals who were highly influential in the 1968 revolt in France. —*Ed.*]

more silent on the question of the imaginary realm and the body, gives us food for thought. Here we may see one of the major reasons why it has suddenly become incumbent upon spectacle* criticism to follow the example of technical criticism—and to do so without us realizing what the latter can actually contribute to the former. In fact, the Situationist vogue, which continues to seduce academic snobbism in the countries that no longer have any resistance to the tyranny of the technical—particularly the United States—is significant, especially because these countries' inopportune evocation helps to disguise an internalization of the technical. This is an irreversible condition resulting from the logic of computers, which have become essential to both work and leisure. It is all the more significant because the "price to pay" for this "new communications system . . . capable of embracing and including all forms of expression, as well as the diversity of interests, values, and imaginations, including the expression of social conflicts," is "adaptation to its logic, its language, its entry points, and its encoding and decoding."[3]

Thus, the denunciation of the image and the denunciation of the spectacle are the latest critical illusions offered to us by society at the very moment when these denunciations cannot explain this new modeling of the world. First, as this world modeling falls far short of the spectacular, it becomes mixed up in the race of frenzied rationalization. In addition, this rationalization results as much from the growing grip of an increasingly aggressive technology as it does from the passivity—or complacency—with which the last two generations of intellectuals have responded to it.

In fact, it would be hard to mistake the role played in this process by the pseudoscientific ideology with which structuralism is coupled, while simultaneously declaring the death of the subject, the disappearance of meaning, and the erasure of history. We may well ask whether the Structuralists, seeking to grasp the mechanism rather than the

*[*The Society of the Spectacle,* written by Guy Debord in 1967. The book implies that society is divided between the passive subjects who consume the spectacle and the reified spectacle itself. —*Ed.*]

meaning and encouraged by the mediocre thinking of the moment, have not acted (albeit subconsciously) as faithful servants of the technocratic society. At the very least, the Structuralists have done a remarkable job of functioning as a conveyor belt. They have used their consultation of linguistics followed by semiotics to place their rationalist grid over everything that through the imaginary dimension of people and things inspires their power of negation.

How can we not be struck by the simultaneity of this clear-cutting of the mental forest with the annihilation of certain South American jungles? How can we help but conclude that the resulting rupture of the great biological balance corresponds to a comparable rupture of the great balance of sensibility in which our thought continues to find sustenance?

3

LIGHT POLLUTION

If, despite the degrading adulation of it, youth can still possess some sort of beauty, then that beauty is that of its despair, for it is youthful despair that is sometimes capable of rekindling those vital questions that the culture strives to reduce to ashes.

We can recall how, not so long ago, those who had suddenly discovered "the deserts of love"[1] turned to Baudelaire, Rimbaud, or Sade,* to mention but a few of those who stand like fortresses against the ludicrous illusion of fair weather. No doubt, anyone who has been exposed to the idiotic refrains of amorous harmony (or rather, amorous complicity) has been tempted to identify with these writers' testimonies. These testimonies, in turn, lead us to assume that the land is never conquered and that our finest gestures emerge from the brutal impossibility of sticking to the status quo.

Nevertheless, once past these initial revolts, which we soon forget out of practical necessity, many people try to delude themselves about what they abandoned so quickly. Unconsciously, for most of them, culture is recognized only as the most elegant function of blindness. Its legitimacy is most often based on the necessity of giving style to things that can have no allure. Never before, however, has society so openly

*[French poets and writers: Charles Baudelaire (1821–1867), Arthur Rimbaud (1854–1891), and the Marquis de Sade (1740–1814). —*Ed.*]

used all its resources to make each individual destiny conform to a reality purified of the slightest element that could cast any doubt upon that reality.

From cultural activities to aesthetic theories, the sole glory of the last ten years is the revelation of the lightning-fast progress achieved in this kind of devastation. The frenzy of various powers investing in the cultural domain makes the phenomenon particularly disturbing—and all the more so because there has been an almost universal mobilization to deforest, flatten, till, cultivate, and map out this domain. Quite naturally, this is where we find the "investors in the mind," whose first concern is to protect a conceptual hold so shaky on its foundations that their differences in laying claim to it, whether for the sake of writing, limits, differences, or humanism, ultimately amount to equivalent strategies. These strategies are motivated essentially by the desire to prevent any threat to their true primary concern, which is the position they occupy in the world.

This development is so pronounced that it is not hard at all to find, in the recent intellectual arsenal, something capable of functioning as a bulldozer, a steam shovel, or a cement mixer for the task of reducing the reserves of unreality, pockets of obscurity, and archipelagoes of shadow. The deleterious atmospheres of these reserves are still capable of casting a matchless disheartening glow upon the progress of a reality that is well on its way to exercising its reconciliatory hegemony.

Thus we have seen linguists, semiologists, sociologists, and psychoanalysts take possession—with the self-importance of specialists—of the very element in the painting and poetry of the nineteenth and twentieth centuries that had scored a direct hit on the order of things. It is also significant that surrealism and its choices have selectively borne the brunt of this appropriation. No longer concealed, as was long the case, these choices have become the raw material for the fabrication of a surrealist aesthetic that has never really existed. The sole aim of this aesthetic: making us forget the fundamental revolt that was the source of the twentieth century's greatest attempt to rethink human beings entirely and to give the prerogative to sensibility.

Hence, the urgent need to do away with surrealism's project of "reimpassioning life" justifies all forms of conscious insubordination, past or future. This insubordination provides the basis for so many invented answers to the sole question worth asking: How do we live? Surrealism, which is not attributable to any kind of theoretical program, is still capable of causing more distress than any other kind of radical approach, precisely because it has wagered everything—disregarding any cultural concern—on the passionate violence of which an individual either is or is not capable.

It hardly matters, then, that only a small number of those who shared in the adventure have been capable of keeping to this wager over the long haul. This wager would presuppose a bettor's profound disinterestedness, contempt for risk, and refusal to compromise. The true danger posed by that small number is their superb contribution to casting a new light upon this quest for meaning, restoring it to its passionate source. Today more than ever, seen in this light from which humans have not yet managed to tear themselves, everything pursued under the pretext of art, literature, or research looks like entertainment. The reason for this, as André Breton rightly spells out in the *Second Surrealist Manifesto:*

> [T]here is not a man whose revolt has been channeled and exhausted who can keep this revolt from rumbling, though there are not as many men as we would wish—and history has hardly been made by their ascension on their knees—who can make this revolt, in its great dark moments, tame the perpetually renascent beast of "this is better."

■

In order to evaluate the wealth of adventures that have resulted from this revolt—and they come to us through personal testimony, texts, and paintings, like so many capsizing, dismasted ships—we can measure the task confronting the cultivated disinformation that now takes the place of cultural authority in all our countries. The response to the initial dismay of this disinformation was a lengthy, patient toil that aimed to erase even the memory of a revolt forever capable of dragging anyone out to the open sea. It is a rule of thumb that these authorities retain only the cultural aspect of what still rumbles in the storms through which we have traveled—which could pop up again as easily as a drifting bottle in the ocean or a ghost ship. It will be no easy task to force these polished or shattered convulsive forms back into the pigeonholes of art history once they have been pulled from the disquieting eddies, stripped of the foam of their incompletion, and finally disengaged from the concretions of despair that enable them to keep their frantic appearance.

I emphasize this because, contrary to what we might think, this is not an artistic problem at all. In fact, it derives from nothing less than the existence of the night: our night, that night to which we all return each evening to live out the best part of our lives. This is what is threatened by this new cultural activism that nothing seems capable of stopping.

Thus, it is alarming to learn that during this same period of time, the Russian Vladimir Syromyatniko, "managing director of the Space Regatta Consortium (SRC), a group of Russian industries formed in 1990," had the idea of preventing night from falling on certain areas of the globe by using satellite lighting. Worse yet, this was recently put into action (similar to what has happened in the cultural domain): On February 3, 1999, the newspaper *Le Monde* announced that with the goal of "bringing light to those regions plunged into polar night," the cosmonauts of Mir were preparing "to deploy a thin aluminum mirror about 26 yards in diameter"—called Znamia (the Standard)—that, like "a giant magnifying glass, would focus a spot of sunlight from five to seven yards in diameter." This spot would "make sweeps over the earth at great speed."

The experiment had been attempted previously, in 1993. It was not very conclusive in 1993 or 1999; but this hardly matters. The true concern is that this Standard against the night continues to orbit above us, and has found promoters on two occasions, despite the protests of astronomers alarmed by the possible exacerbation of "light pollution" caused by cities and an increasing number of satellites.

But worst of all, what still seems difficult to achieve with cosmic night is well on its way to success in terms of mental night. From the perspective of sensibility, there is a kind of light pollution that is even more formidable, because it threatens directly all the dark components of our freedom. What's more, this light pollution, aimed at achieving total illumination, implies an objectification of all the zones of shadow—and this can lead only to the confusion of reality and positivism.

Thanks to the constant progress of this artificial lighting of the shadow zones, André Breton's beast of "this is better" has been able to prosper as never before—so much so that it struts about today in the pastures of an increasingly triumphant reality. For a long while now, most people have thought themselves secure enough to attempt the domestication of irreducible spirits such as Lautréamont, Sade, Rimbaud, and Artaud* to the extent that every intellectual whose name is even slightly recognized has attempted to harness to these spirits his or her own patented rationalizing interpretation. In addition, many university theses, excruciating in their pretentious falsity, have been inspired by these examples. Today, the combined efforts of textual modernity and the modernity of computer technology make it evident that this rationalization has become the most effective instrument of alienation.

We use whatever light we can; our era will be lit by light pollution.

*[In addition to the French writers the Marquis de Sade and Arthur Rimbaud, the comte de Lautréamont (Isidore Lucien Ducasse, 1846–1870) and Antonin Artaud (1896–1948). —*Ed.*]

4

THE STERILE HORIZON

The fact that this light pollution seems self-evident to almost everyone would smack of the mysterious if we did not consider the desertification to which the apparently contradictory tendencies of the post-Structuralist philosophy of the last ten years have contributed. Indeed, we should remember that in order to reach this point, everything belonging to the sensorial domain has been subjected to an intense theorization process. This theorization process is comparable to the excessive clear-cutting that modifies "the physical characteristics of the ground surface" by increasing "its potential to reflect back into space solar radiation and the evaporation caused by plants" in such a way that "the sterilization that results from its negative effects accentuates these effects . . ."[1] This is the same kind of vicious circle that, through the impoverishment of our surroundings, has governed the production of a pseudo-literature by the very same individuals who invented its theory. In a similar fashion, in the realm of the plastic arts, artists who distinguish themselves by an unprecedented, submissive attitude toward cultural politics and institutional strategies have irremediably altered the artistic landscape merely through their occupation of it.

This kind of devastation could not have reached its current amplitude if, in 1971, Roland Barthes, when comparing Sade, Fourier, and Loyola as "founders of a language" and "nothing more than that . . . specifically to say nothing, to observe a vacancy," had not come to the conclusion that "the center, the weight, and the meaning have been dismissed." This disquieting fact has succeeded in cretinizing an entire generation or two, forewarning us of the innumerable conveniences offered by this liquidation of meaning, which authorizes us to speak both to say nothing and to say everything in order to do anything. In fact, if "Sade is no longer an eroticist, Fourier is no longer a utopian, and Loyola is no longer a saint."[2] Nothing has any meaning at all anymore—and the ensuing equality of insignificance makes the singularity of each individual, author, or reader equally meaningless.

Just for kicks, I include this remark made by Novalis: "Strange that there is not yet any moral legislation concerning the duties of readers and the rights of authors."

In order to shed some light upon our now sterile horizon, we can also recall that Roland Barthes, famous as a lover of language, had no qualms about declaring in his inaugural lecture at the Collège de France that "our language, like the performance of any language, is neither reactionary nor progressive; it is simply fascist, because fascism does not mean preventing someone from speaking. It means coercing someone to speak."[3] Consequently, considering that in conditions of desertification "only a small proportion of the plants and animals that lived initially in the affected habitat can survive in a barren landscape,"[4] it is easier to imagine why nothing has been able to oppose the originators of a similar process in the realm of ideas and forms. This comprises both the "deconstructionists" who followed the originators, advancing the idea that in the final analysis neither text nor image means anything, and the opposing "pragmatists," who recognize that the smallest sign can mean anything. In reality, both groups are on the same side in the battle against meaning, which, despite their claims, has them working together toward the annihilation of all critical thought, along with the rejection of the sensorial dimension that makes it possible.

■

Recent trends have even given us grounds to think that this is the direction history is taking, at least if we can go by the sight of writers, philosophers, professors, art critics, and journalists all scurrying in the same direction. But we should not be surprised by this kind of activity; it has been duly recognized as a public service. How could this world not be grateful to those who have accepted jobs as informants in regions where there still remains something that is not quantifiable, measurable, and reducible to some kind of norm? And if there falls to those same informants the task of replacing great sensorial adventures with substitutes tolerated by this society, then they will be rewarded by promotion to the rank of omniscient consultants. This is only right, for they have spent a full decade working to neutralize everything in the cultural realm that might constitute a danger of subversion—and this new intellectual class has thus produced the most zealous justifiers of the status quo.

In this regard, the reopening of the Pompidou Center, which was renovated at the beginning of the year 2000, forms both an apotheosis and a point of no return. This was echoed even more loudly by the concert of praise from the press that greeted the restarting of this gigantic mixer of force-fed cultural reality excess. Yet no one has been able to explain just why this Pompidou overhaul was a good idea, except that it made the center more cheerful, more transparent, and more multidisciplinary. No doubt, the era saw its own reflection in the renovators' concern for maintaining a lack of differentiation. This concern seems to have presided over the renovation, which, among other things, aimed "not to build in a too conveniently amnesiac manner, not to erect contemporaneity in a fleeting moment having neither yesterday nor tomorrow, neither roots nor result," as the museum's president, Jean-Jacques Aillagon, explained in a text entitled *Un Siècle, un musée, un regard* [One Age, One Museum, One View].[5] The little that can be deciphered from this pretentious hodgepodge of a book does reveal that the desire to place this institution within the orbit of modernity appears to have been the main principle behind this renovation. The result looks more like a highway interchange than a panorama of modern art.

There are some metaphors that cannot deceive. Any doubts on this point are dispelled by the profession of faith that Werner Spies, the director of this new national museum of modern art, made in response to a journalist who brought up the danger of "museumizing" contemporary creations:

> We have adopted the principle of a museum with several different speeds: a historical speed in the first section of the exhibition, where the works have been canonized or are in the process of becoming so; and a second speed for the more contemporary works. The closer we get to the present day, the less we can judge the artists' value in a definitive fashion. So it is much more fair to keep changing the displays. It is as if the young artists are here on a trial basis.[6]

We already had "information superhighways." What we were missing were circuit boards of culture—but now that's taken care of. This is the likely reason why the various critics who observed the opening of the Pompidou seem to have remembered especially the descriptive plaques revised to suit current tastes: They seem to have been revised in such a way that those who make a habit of visiting museums on the Internet will be entirely in their element. They present modern art as an "excursion" modeled on a computer network, allowing the viewer to glide from one work to the next, with an obvious emphasis placed on circulation, like a cultural application of the well-known command: "Move along, there's nothing to see here." Although the initiator of these "excursions" strives to convince us that "the approach taken here is the establishment of a web of understanding,"[7] we cannot help but doubt the truth of this statement once the mighty idea that allegedly inspired this revolutionary artistic approach finally hits us: "[C]ontemporary art succeeds indubitably by the reading of what preceded it. It has no place beyond history."[8]

This is why we must not underestimate the fact that most of these ideas are taken from a work glorifying such a rereading of modernity. Indeed, the title *Une Histoire matérielle* [A Material History] betrays the mania of objectification that has replaced reflection in this new museography, which is eager to catch in its snare of reality primarily anything that, by nature, normally escapes it. With regard to this, I can remain silent no longer: What has been presented to us as the event to top all events—the installation of an "almost identical" wall from André Breton's studio "at the heart of the museum"—in fact constitutes the most depressing example of this phenomenon.

"This had been a fantasy of the museum heads for a long time,"[9] recalls Werner Spies, failing to see the degree to which such a fantasy is an indicator of this new museography, whose tendency is less to collect artworks and more to collect the greatest possible quantity of elements in order to fabricate pieces of reality that encroach more and more on imaginary space. The craze for "installations," which have become the art of our time, is the most flagrant proof of this. In the case of this wall from André Breton's studio, the transition from fantasy to its realization takes on a highly symbolic value.

Whoever did not have the good fortune to experience André Breton's studio personally, to enter that interior, can refer to Julien Gracq's description of it. In his beautiful text from *En lisant, en écrivant* [Reading and Writing]—which the makers of this "installation" undoubtedly did not read, and if they had, the result would be even worse—Julien Gracq first speaks of how "the profusion of art objects hanging everywhere on the walls had gradually shrunk the available space; movement was possible only on precise pathways formed by use, and these paths avoided the branches, vines, and thorns of a forest path."

Of course, nothing remains of this forest in the installation's hanging of two hundred and fifty objects (and not a single opportunity is missed to draw attention to this considerable number) displayed behind an immense pane of glass. This is a vivisection of the interlacing of future dreams and thoughts that had once evolved from each other and from, as Gracq recalls, "the heavy table that looked like a counter," where Breton would sit. It was "a goldsmith's or money changer's table, seeming to summon around it the heavy pelisses that inhabit the half-light of Rembrandt's paintings. . . ."

In vain we search for any sign of this presence that Julien Gracq, ten years after Breton's death, still felt so strongly in this organic dwelling—a presence that mirrored the shape of a thought that reinvented its space by forcing reality to give way to the starlike fracturing of the perspectives of everything that does not exist. "Here there was a refuge against everything mechanical in the world," Julien Gracq says in conclusion. Unfortunately, simply taking one section from this refuge has annihilated it. From the poetic point of view, this reveals a serious omission; but evidently the current administrators of art do not have the slightest idea of this, even if Breton dealt with just this subject in *Signe ascendant* [Rising Sign], when he recalled the Zen koan in which the disciple says: "Take a dragonfly, tear off its wings: a pimento." To which his master responds, "No, take a pimento, give it wings: a dragonfly."

Accordingly, in the same way that the disciple has no qualms about killing a dragonfly to display his highly dubious poetic savoir-faire, the cultural experts of the Pompidou Center, under the pretext of revealing more, have had no hesitation in tearing Breton's wall from everything that gave it life, beginning with his strong sense of insubordination that presided over the passionate choice of these objects—themselves not so much objects of art as objects of passion, and each testifying in its own way to a ferocious refusal to stick to what is presented as reality.

By all evidence, it is precisely a result of this mutilation that seems to so satisfy Werner Spies when he declares: "The curiosity cabinet aspect of the collection is almost a bedazzlement."[10] It is remarkable that this bedazzlement that isn't a bedazzlement (just what is "almost bedazzlement"?) compares so completely to the pimento that isn't a pimento about which the Zen disciple brags after a similar mutilation. Breton endowed these objects with an unprecedented new life by choosing them deliberately against this world's intellectual and artistic tastes and values, and then by placing them together outside all recognized criteria—just as the Zen master, giving wings to a simple pimento, suddenly imparts life to a brand-new dragonfly. I cannot help thinking that this brand-new dragonfly took flight when Breton placed Cazal's staggering portrait of Alfred Jarry next to an anthropomorphic Mexican ax from the Mezcal culture, thereby conjuring the charged despair of the one through the metaphorical violence of the other. And such effects go on, object by object, in the most splendid entanglement of sensorial life reinventing itself against everything that seeks to subjugate it.

Because there will be plenty of well-meaning individuals and clever intellectuals to justify the disastrous misinterpretation that has presided over the display of these surrealist relics from an antielitist point of view, it is perhaps worth recalling the contempt in which Breton held all public recognition. He took pains to emphasize this in the *Second Surrealist Manifesto:* "Public approval must be avoided above all else. The public must be strictly forbidden from *entering* if we are to avoid confusion."

We cannot help but note that the confusion has reached its apogee today. And our cultural experts take advantage of the situation to advance pedagogical arguments that camouflage their grave poetic insufficiencies and the fact that they are still wrong. Everything leads us to believe that they will never understand Breton's conviction that "in matters of revolt, none of us should have a need for ancestors." This cannot be taught.

I only wish that for some people, what I am saying will not be a foreign language—for this would be a sign that those who claim to guide our tastes and dreams and who now form a cultural *nomenklatura* with its own powers, privileges, and impunity have not yet triumphed completely.

As for possible exceptions, it is quite difficult to find any in a time when there is not a single intellectual capable of conceiving the honor of refusing a Medal of Honor. Of course, there are still poets and artists, but we can see from afar how they shove and jostle each other at the trough while trying to grab prizes, medals, and other degrading tokens. Unfortunately, this is not another story.

5

RECONDITIONING CULTURE

Almost three centuries ago, in his *Letter of Advice to a Young Poet,* Jonathan Swift noted: "Although we have not one masterly poet, yet we abound with wardens and beadles; having a multitude of poetasters, poetitoes, parcel-poets, poet-apes, and philo-poets, and many of inferior attainments in wit, but strong inclinations to it, which are by odds more than all the rest." He concluded:

> What if our government had a poet laureate here [Ireland], as in England? What if our university had a professor of poetry here, as in England? What if our lord mayor had a city bard here, as in England? And, to refine upon England, what if every corporation, parish, and ward in this town, had a poet in fee, as they have not in England? Lastly, what if every one, so qualified, were obliged to add one more than usual to the number of his domestics, and beside a fool and chaplain (which are often united in one person) would retain a poet in his family; for perhaps, a rhymer is as necessary among servants of a house as a Dobbin with his bell at the head of a team.

Is there no stopping progress? It seems unlikely, when everything Swift invented from the depths of his gleeful maliciousness appears to be falling short of the truth today.

As for artists—from whom there is not much to expect, judging by what Jacques Vaché* said in 1917: "We don't like art or artists"—there is no telling what might have prevented them from joining the ranks of these cultural domestics. Had they not joined, the title of artist would not be claimed by such a plethora of alleged cultural laborers, who produce today's art to the rhythm of the prizes and grants bestowed upon them so generously by governments worldwide.

In this regard, these new "employees" [cultural laborers] differ not a whit from their professor-poet, professor-painter, and professor-artist colleagues who constitute the proliferating avant-garde of those who are no longer capable of perceiving the fundamental contradiction that is the organizing principle of their existence as specialists in neutralization. They are equally incapable of evaluating the extent to which covering up this contradiction—testified to by each day of their lives—forms part of this communications swindle, whose primary objective is immunization against anything that could be the expression of protest or refusal.

The novelty of this communication swindle is contained entirely in an unprecedented collusion between art and power. This involves a transformation so profound that the most serious art historians today find it impossible not to touch upon this unheard-of phenomenon, which has also drawn the attention of sociologists. The reason is that "unlike premodern eras, which subjected artists to the censure of their patrons, and unlike the modern era, which portrayed the emancipated and subversive artist as the victim of a generally obtuse society, contemporary society strives to institutionalize revolt and make subversion and state subsidies coexist."[1]

But are those who analyze this phenomenon using the excuse of objective neutrality to avoid coming to grips with it? Or is it a sign that reality has already triumphed over anything that could cast doubt upon it, and none of these analysts truly contests the idea that "the misun-

*[Jacques Vaché (1895–1919) exerted a great influence on his friend André Breton and the early surrealists. —*Trans.*]

derstanding of art by its contemporaries and the sacrifice of artists is a situation nobody wants in principle"?[2]

True, art critic Catherine Millet has noted that as "better informed and more tolerant contemporaries seek to place more and more collective spaces at the disposal of artists . . . the model of the marginal or cursed figure becomes proportionately blurry. Those 'suicided by society'* make way for those who are subsidized by society."[3] Millet gives as an example the contradictions of Daniel Buren (who, after gaining notoriety in the 1960s along with several other artists considered enemies of the establishment, later became one of its most faithful servants, executing the commission of the famous Palais Royale columns and serving as director of the École des Beaux-Arts). She asks eventually: "If everything in museographical society is planned out to place, preserve, and advertise the creations of the artist, what part can it still grant to Utopia?"[4] The answer is none, of course.

But the fact remains that while some of these observers have no hesitation in speaking of "an era in which the social position of the artist is no longer that of the outcast poet, but is increasingly that of the sociocultural coordinator,"[5] none of them seems truly shocked by this new dependency of creative work on institutions; they all seem openly inclined to view it as an unavoidable phenomenon. It is even implicitly accepted that "by managing the exhibition space, [those individuals] have a controlling interest in what has become one of the most important means of expression in contemporary art."[6] And it occurs to no one to rebel against the fact that "henceforth, *creation* will be performed, so to speak, in cooperation between the administrators of a space and the tailors of that space, which is what artists have become."[7]

Nor has anyone noticed the crudely obvious manner in which we are led to confuse art and reality. Just as information transmitted "in real time" plays upon "the pseudoevidence of the senses,"[8] suspending reflection and thereby constituting one of the surest means of disinformation, so also we are forced to witness a creation *in real space,* where

*[Reference to Antonin Artaud's *Van Gogh, le suicidé de la société. —Ed.*]

the deceit consists of playing simultaneously on false sensorial evidence and on reality overload in places conceived to win terrain from our imaginary space.

This is surely why the debate on contemporary art, which has been agitating a sector of the intellectual class since 1991, smacks primarily of a masquerade, even though attempts have been made to portray it as an "art war." Art and artists are strangely absent from this art war; under cover of a struggle between the "old guard" (defenders of tradition, skilled workmanship, and deep roots) and the "moderns" (proponents of an avant-garde doctrine that is self-perpetuating for obvious reasons), what is truly at stake is the effort to define the prevailing criteria for determining the distribution of commissions, grants, and prizes. The multiplicity of interventions and the virulence of the debate seem to have no objective other than their displacement in order to avoid any question that this new presentation of art in real space, as required by its regional and national promoters, is *the* representation of our times.

So we must not let ourselves be fooled by the political twists and turns taken by the polemic (the traditionalists playing the role of right-wingers or outright "fascists" and the moderns becoming leftists or outright "Stalinists"), because the

> . . . phenomenon of the anticipated recognition of the avant-garde by institutional power, which we have just experienced over the last fifteen years, has deprived the avant-garde of its anti-institutional dimension, thereby making it possible to combine in one fell swoop avant-garde rejection of the traditionalists with power's customary rejection of the progressives.[9]

This can also be seen in the fact that the most virulent protagonists, Jean Clair (for traditional art) and Philippe Dagen (for contemporary art), are each defending positions diametrically opposed to those they held several years earlier. How can we not come away from this with the impression of a battle whose sole purpose is the conquest of a battlefield?

From this perspective, we can better understand the violent nature of the confrontations, which seem far from ending now that the museum has been given responsibility to function as a display window whose exemplary value is allegedly an aid to the diffusion of this culture in real space. It is as if what is shown within the confines of the museum establishment is intended solely to extend itself to cover the entire sensorial domain. If we are to believe the specialists, it is with the purpose of "manufacturing a social bond" that this "process of requisition and reception of projects and realizations of contemporary public art in France has become the strong point of a state-led operation to aestheticize society."[10] And this process is taken farther afield by local authorities, thanks to the decentralization of power.

Here is a truly reassuring redefinition of the artistic adventure. Too bad that van Gogh, Rimbaud, and several others could not have been our contemporaries. They, who never found their hands in their "age of hands,"* would have been "manufacturers of social bonds" or "aestheticians of society"! We are at risk of forgetting that "domination has its own aesthetic[,] and democratic domination has a democratic aesthetic,"[11] as Herbert Marcuse noted more than thirty years ago. He also points out that by virtue of the ensuing diffusion, "the fine arts are becoming cogs in a cultural machine that remodels their content."[12] Even worse, the machine alters their nature, and consequently the perception of everything that has preceded them.

Such is the dreadful retroactive effect of this reconditioning of culture, whose aim is to influence not only the future of the imaginary realm, but also the past, from which it has drawn nourishment since time immemorial.

---

*[A reference to Rimbaud's poem "Mauvais Sang" (Bad Blood): "Quel siècle à mains!—Je n'aurai jamais ma main" ("What an age of hands!—I'll never have my hand"). —*Ed.*]

In this regard, novelty is considerable, for, bizarrely, until these last few decades—out of fear, incomprehension, or simple instinctive self-preservation—the bourgeoisie had kept their distance. Just as they had been able to hold on for a long time (at least for their own enjoyment) to various landscapes and realms (thanks to an ancient sense of moderation), so also they had felt it better not to meddle too much in what came out of the mental forest. They were content merely with occasionally buying something and bringing out from it a marvel they did not know how to obtain themselves. It was not until the notion of conservation arose—born jointly from the passion of the collector and the rigorous concepts of the museum and library—that a paradoxical space, relatively protected from control or exploitation, could be erected around objects and texts, thereby guaranteeing their authenticity and integrity.

Analogically, all forms of expression benefit at least a little from this status, provided they do not directly draw the attention of the censor and the ever-watchful moral order. When this has not been possible, as was the case for Baudelaire with *Les Fleurs du mal* (The Flowers of Evil) or for the surrealists with the first screenings of *L'Âge d'or,** the offending object was attacked. It was forbidden—but not neutralized, disarmed, or adulterated, as happens today through the multiplicity of cultural usages and the proliferation of research centers, foundations, and museums (whose sole objective is to make everything equivalent).

This titanic task (to make everything equivalent) required, as we know, a mob of cultural experts who reduce the history of our sensibility to nothing more or less than a data bank. Of course, it was not necessary to wait for the Internet to reach this point. In fact, that mode of communication is merely a well-adapted instrument that aims at the rational mastery of all those things within each of us that still resist this project of total domination. Not only is everything—impressions,

*[Luis Buñuel's and Salvador Dali's second film collaboration, *L'Âge d'or* (The Golden Age), was attacked by right-wing protesters, who destroyed the screening room and artwork displayed in the cinema showing it. —*Trans.*]

feelings, desires—meant to become marketable merchandise; from this point of view, the boutiques adjoining our museums, which are increasingly rich in gadgets and videos, are not fundamentally any different from sex shops. Also, gridlike division of the sensorial space is the best means for installing a borderless conformity as a guarantor of servitude accepted on a worldwide scale.

We can note that this limitless expansion into space—which tends to impose the swindle of a creation in real space—goes hand in hand with a compression that results from crushing the historical perspective. Whether it consists of the presentation of the works of an individual, of a group, or of an era, time always disappears beneath the abundance of pieces and documents accumulated for the purpose of convincing us that the question has been totally exhausted. In other words, this informational glut prevents us from seeing the play of presences and absences that nonetheless continue to connect us to the past as well as to the present, and induce us to share a little of our own darkness with history. It is precisely this quality that makes us increasingly incapable of perceiving any distinctions between the countless exhibitions, monographs, and biographies that give the illusion of having assembled every possible scrap of data on any subject.

Ample evidence of this can be found in the impressive weight of those books and catalogs in which empty moments and crucial times, minor productions and essential gestures, simple anecdotes and important testimonies are all placed on an equal level. The remarkable arrival of a being, for instance, is counterbalanced systematically by the outcome of his or her simple human condition. We have only to look at how, with one exhumation after another of insignificant papers, some have attempted to make us forget the dazzling quality of Jacques Vaché's *War Letters.** In the same way, the arrival and disappearance of Arthur Cravan† in broad

*[Jacques Vaché's *War Letters* is a posthumous book about surrealist antimilitarism and subversion. —*Ed.*]

†[Arthur Cravan (1887–1918), a larger-than-life character and poet, was an idol of the surrealist movement. He mysteriously disappeared off the coast of Mexico. —*Ed.*]

daylight is undoubtedly too radiant for people not to try to conceal that light beneath a heap of documents and critical commentaries.

Finally, we cannot ignore the suffocation that has presided over the exhibition devoted to the self-taught painter Gaston Chaissac. In this exhibition, the accumulation of works of often uneven quality ended up hobbling the free appearance of the artist's creatures, whose singular strength resides in their emergence from daily life in energetic masses that invent movement like a child's game.

But it is useless to continue in this vein; the production of these cultural packages has become so routine. Far from being innocent, they contribute to the internalization of a liquidation of history that is much subtler than the classic methods to which totalitarian governments have resorted. Here, we do not erase; we accumulate, we overinform—all the better to dismember. What is the good of thinking that impressionism has some relationship to symbolism when these are two distinct "products," two distinct "entries"? And yet this proves to be no obstacle. Our stage directors have accustomed us to seeing the Nazi era and the Elizabethan age, antiquity and Vienna 1900 rub shoulders.

But far be it from anyone to imagine an analogical reason for such concertinaing. This new fashion of destroying history, through which lies postmodernism's originality, aims at replacing a coherence that gives meaning with a juxtaposition that causes shock. Thus crushed, the historical perspective can easily be recycled in space, where all that remains to be done is to insert it into a series of interchangeable backdrops. Here, all eras, all cultures, all landscapes are within reach. This accustoms us, in our heart of hearts, to a world that seeks to make us confuse freedom with the obligation that it lays upon us to avoid making any connection among facts, ideas, and individuals.

Those who might think it still possible to recover something by using what has always connected us to our world—language—are barking mad. Language, that strange treasure we make our own only through sharing, is something we are in the process of losing.

6

A WIDESPREAD TWISTING AROUND

Arthur Cravan said that genius needs horns to protect itself. No doubt, though, he was completely unaware of the invention that two policemen bumped up against on January 8, 1910. They were trying to arrest a thin young man who, on the say-so of a stoolie, had been talking at the "Caves moderne" about "knocking off a cop." As the bells of Saint-Merri* rang out at 8:30, thinking they recognized in the shadows the individual they sought, the policemen tackled him, only to let him go immediately while they screamed in pain, their hands covered with blood. Underneath his cape, on his biceps and forearms, the young anarchist Jean-Jacques Liaboeuf wore leather armbands studded with long, sharp spikes.

Thinkers of any intensity must be equipped with devices of this kind in order to avoid apprehension. Despite, or because of, the serious airs they assume, manners of speaking exist that are much less armed than they appear. For example, Guy Debord failed to prevent Philippe Sollers—followed by all the underlings of arts and letters—from invoking Debord's name today to the point of obscenity. This occurred even though Debord himself took the trouble to emphasize how "insignificant" something appeared to him "because it was signed PHILIPPE SOLLERS."[1] The above event refers to the oration to Debord

*[A small church in central Paris. —*Ed.*]

that Sollers, the former 1960s Maoist and/or Stalinist who has since become a festive papist and a Balladurian* of a libertine bent, rushed to deliver in the November 5, 1992, edition of *L'Humanité*.†

It would be nice to believe that Guy Debord, who wished to be the "extreme artist" of *détournement,*§ did not himself fall victim to such a wretched *détournement*. But this sinister passing fad may still provide a timely opportunity for muddying the waters still more, thus illustrating how insidiously, over the last decade, language has allowed itself to undergo a *twist* (in the detective-novel sense of the term).

This would hardly be the first time that words have been used for the purpose of deception, but something in their nature is in the process of being altered under the pressure of a world that gradually forces a language to substitute itself for ideas, feelings, and opinions—all of which are found lacking in comparison to an increasingly invasive reality.

The most gripping example of this substitution is provided by the invention of *bioethics,* in which the sudden overload of biological reality, including the envisaging of a genetically engineered humanity, has led to a language that has permitted "the filling of a generalized social anomie," as noted by the psychoanalyst Monette Vacquin.[2]

From plumbing to linguistics, from data processing to do-it-yourself guides, from the lottery to typography, and so on, words and expressions have been borrowed with a fever that speaks volumes about the novelty of a situation in which "while our subjective certainties are collapsing one by one—our certainty of the necessary and beneficial alienation of the sexes in parenthood; of being born of one woman . . . ; of being unique and nonreplicable; and of being contained within a stable reality or its

---

*[Édouard Balladur is a right-wing politician and former prime minister of France (1993–1995) who left office to mount an unsuccessful campaign to become president of France. —*Trans.*]

†[*L'Humanité* is the official organ of the French Communist Party. —*Trans.*]

§[*Détournement* is a genre of art, pioneered by Guy Debord, in which existing media are reworked to convey a new, often subversive message. The term could be translated as "misappropriation" or "twisting around." —*Ed.*]

nearest equivalent and being shielded from personal follies—a language has been successfully imposed upon us in less than ten years."[3] In this way, "expressions extending from *planned parenthood* to the *planned parenthood of others* by means of *embryo storage* and *embryonic reduction* have enjoyed great success by virtue of their ability to be meaningless and freeze the imagination with their abstract nature and power to overwhelm."[4]

In other words, because of our want of being able to conceive of this reality overload now spreading over the deepest reaches of our inner life, it was left to language to cover all the contributions of technoscience, the idea being that these terms would spare us actually having to think about this kind of technology. Without the airing of a single criticism, a stupefying linguistic accord has been grafted onto expressions launched like advertising slogans—expressions that are capable of moving from a jaunty transgression (inaugurated by *test-tube babies*) to the efficiency of management in evoking, for example, a new legal status and legal terminology for individuals as *parents of frozen embryos.*

We can now say whatever we like, on condition it is accompanied by high-flown and well-meaning references to a *professional code of ethics,* the *dignity of the human being,* and so on, with apotheoses in the *freedom of research* achieved with the *desire to have a baby,* or vice versa. It is as if the more we venture into a night of haphazard identities, uncertain affiliations, and improbable personalities, and the harder we strain our voice, the drunker words make us. This has become so excessive that "if one catastrophe occurred during the decade preceding passage of the so-called bioethic laws, it concerned language above all."[5]

We might say this is an extreme example if we couldn't note a similar pressure placed upon language in a number of other areas. Although many of these instances take on the appearance of opposite forms, all provide equal proof of the brutality with which our excessive reality suddenly weighs upon the universe of words that allegedly serves to explain it.

Scarcely anyone seems to be worried by the fact that this manifests itself in a multitude of equally monstrous and ridiculous innovations, such as *optimizing, positioning, profitability, dangerousness,* and *employability,* which can easily compete with *giving things a positive spin, sponsoring, feasibility, reputable,* and *impacting.* Nor is anyone worried by the fact that this kind of innovation—which traps words within a single definition—is always paid for by a loss of the plasticity to which they owed their wealth of meaning until now. By having only one meaning, how could a word not become more rigid? Each would then wear the definitive uniform of a single function, like soldiers or specialists.

Conversely, there are words used to say anything and everything, and from this overuse, they become callous before going on to become the components of hackneyed phrases. Among these are: *culture, solidarity, diversity, nation, communication, dialogue. . . .* It could even be said that under the pressure of a reality whose excess also consists of having a name for everything, there has been a thickening of a word's texture, which goes on to conquer the entire language until, increasingly, it takes on the tone of something assumed.* We need consider this only briefly to come away with the disagreeable impression that the terms we use are less words than they are assumed names. In the same way, a multitude of concepts are summoned to appear in new places, such as *pants concept, hairstyle concept,* and *culinary concept.* These constructs loom one after the other with a comical precipitation that conceals how such systematic recourse to these kinds of misleading approximations amounts to a decisive stage in the twisting of words.

This situation is already so advanced that most people do not even appear to see how words, by losing at the same time their flexibility and their specificity, have been gradually reduced to a new status as extras whose role is to conceal the absence of what they once meant.

We might also consider those *creative centers* where nothing is cre-

*[The French word for "assume," *emprunter,* can also mean "to borrow" or "to feign." —*Trans.*]

ated and those *research centers* where nothing is sought or found. . . . There are so many examples with which we are all familiar. Their proliferation makes this new mania for naming what no longer exists, or what never existed, still more disturbing. Even more alarming is one of the effects of this harassment of language by a reality that is increasingly hostile to anything that is not exclusively self-referential: its specific attack against ideas, values, and feelings.

Examples of this are as numerous as they are depressing. If *freedom* is mentioned, it is to disguise its absence. If the words *love* and *desire* are uttered, even for antagonistic purposes, merely considering who is speaking will be enough to convince us that we do not want to know what kind of nonsense or derisory cynicism the speaker is trying to put over on us. As for poetry, if all we had were the poets of the recent *fin de siècle* to give that word meaning, I would be perfectly ready to regard it as a synonym for posing, emptiness, pusillanimity, self-importance, incontinence, turgidity, and, in the final analysis, profound dishonesty.

But I will deliberately refrain from drawing up a list of such examples that are repeated daily—a list of all those words that still display an air of being present and are suddenly found absent, like the missing step on a staircase. The fact remains that such changes could not help but affect our innermost depths. Everything points to the equivalence of word gymnastics and the manipulations that have resulted in *genetically modified organisms.* In the same way that grains and vegetables are tampered with under the pretext of making them more pest resistant—a justifiable cause for alarm because of the unknown dangers this tampering may create—among the words that we are led to believe are still capable of provoking excitement, there are no longer any that are not actively working against the ideas they allegedly express.

But often we do not know what taboo seems to prohibit people from perceiving this growing inadequacy of language to describe what is taking place, along with the overexertion and "steroid enhancement" of those terms that are often used to the point of exhaustion in an environment that is increasingly foreign to their history. How can we even imagine the intensive efforts to which words such as *ethical, deontological,* and *memory* must have been subjected in order to retain some semblance of meaningfulness, even though they might be deprived of their daily nourishment? How can we comprehend the artificially maintained survival of a word such as *transparency,* which smacks of pure provocation against a horizon that every day grows foggier in the realms of business and ideas alike?

In less than ten years, language has become so much a shadow of itself that it can no longer even cast shadows. I do not know if, in the history of expression, the uncertainty of the ends has ever been so outrageously dependent upon that of the means.

7

THE WORD AS FALSE WITNESS

Yet belief in language is such that in the end, this belief becomes lost. Whatever may be said, each of us remains convinced (a century after Freud's discoveries, which each of us believes apply to everyone but us) that we own our language like we own our money: We hoard meaning and value alike without questioning what personal or collective interests are obeyed by the property we believe we own—even when it is obvious to everyone else that we are merely its unconscious conveyor. Accordingly, it was not enough that the surrealists in the 1920s staked their hopes on a language freed from the control imposed upon it by usage in order to create, as Alfred Jarry dreamed of earlier, "a crossroads of *all* the words on the highway of sentences." It was not enough that this small group of young people then charged headlong into a plan to take words at their word, so that these words might start speaking without anyone taking away their voice: "And may it be thoroughly understood that when we say word games, it is our surest reasons to live that are at play. Besides, words have stopped playing. Words are making love."

Perhaps it was too much when not only rationalist imbecility found itself threatened, but also all rational wording was placed suddenly at the mercy of what language clandestinely brings forth from itself. It is remarkable that any theoretical endeavor of importance—with, of course, the exception of certain speculations confined to the psychoanalytical realm—has regarded the revelation of this dark forest as null and void. Nevertheless, this forest continues to run alongside the borders of the most controlled thought trends. Impatient to make us see this for ourselves, Michel Leiris spilled the beans in 1925 in the opening of *Glossaire: j'y serre mes gloses* [Glossary: Where I Lock My Glosses]: "A monstrous aberration has given men the impression that language was born to facilitate their mutual relations." Nothing came of his attempt; people instead preferred to get rid of this disagreeable discovery, behaving as if we should leave literature to the literati.

An implicit new order flowed out of this attempt, with the aim of reducing each word to the role of a simple hireling, though it was still recognized that language's experimental practices had the right to some freedom. The word was brought to heel as discreetly and efficiently as possible, which was no doubt intentional but nevertheless indicative of the defensive reaction of a world subconsciously troubled about its foundations.

Perhaps the reason for this new order is attributable to the stupefying libertarian eloquence that took place two decades earlier—as beautiful as a firedamp explosion in the labyrinths of contingency—and that came less from anarchist intellectuals than from high-flying thieves and bomb planters, the fractious and "rebellious" of every stripe who endowed language with the most natural forms of sovereignty. The fact remains that from Émile Paget, founder of *Père Peinard,* to Louis Lecoin, by way of Marius Jacob, there was a general participation in a reappropriation of language on the part of those whose social status had kept them at a distance from all culture at first. We can equate this to the "individual repossession" practiced by the Night Workers,* organized by Marius Jacob, who, between 1897 and 1905, retrieved from castles, churches, and villas "a little of what their owners had stolen."

Humor and grandeur thus found themselves neighbors in a lan-

*[*Les Travailleurs de la nuit* (the Night Workers) were a gang of anarchist burglars in France led by Marius Jacob around the beginning of the twentieth century. —*Ed.*]

guage that sometimes earned even the honors of the press. Their extreme coherence of opinions and gestures gave insolence a certain hitherto unknown air of nobility, which would have an influence on the finest minds at the junction of the nineteenth and twentieth centuries. This includes (among others) Darien* and Jarry, who were able to send echoing from their innermost depths a language transmuted by the brute force of insubordination that was inseparable from life taking back its rights throughout the history of the anarchist revolt. The air of Paris [during this junction] retained that keen nonchalance and agility that takes possession of both ideas and bodies, giving them an appearance of natural defiance. Until around the 1960s, among a certain number of its artisans and workers, as well as in many cafés, this city remained the host of a language capable of making the spirit of the times a perpetually renewed bridge to the night of the great refusal.

Around this same time, atomic fallout became a cause for alarm for many people, but those concerned about the fallout affecting language from the technological choices made by our societies were few in number. No one seemed to notice the analogical way in which these two kinds of fallout struck telling blows upon our ways of living and thinking. Furthermore, as dark as all the forecasts may have been, none dared imagine the scope of the current desolation.

Despite the rationalist limitations of his positions, Herbert Marcuse, in his *One-Dimensional Man* (1964), deserves to be acknowledged as first to raise the alarm about the dangers of a "new conformism, which is a facet of technological rationality."[1] In his view, this new social behavior, "rational to an unprecedented degree," was in the process of "closing the universe of discourse" and reducing speech to an object, the signified to the signifier, and the word to a "publicized and standardized" content.[2]

*[Georges Darien, pen name of Georges Adrien (1862–1921), best known as the author of the novels *Le Voleur* (The Thief) and *Bas les Coeurs!* (Lower Your Hearts!), as well as the polemical pamphlet *La Belle France*. —*Trans.*]

Nevertheless, because each individual believed himself sole master at the helm of language, little attention was paid to this state of affairs. This made it all the easier to forget that language is a living organism that is nourished by what it absorbs. And it is an organism whose vitality depends especially on whether or not its absorptive abilities become a transformational power. The French language of the second half of the eighteenth century, Elizabethan English, late-eighteenth-century German, twelfth-century Italian, and the French language of the junction of the nineteenth and twentieth centuries all resulted from this subtle and grandiose alchemy. This is the point at which language gives thought the additional energy to allow it to venture beyond itself, generating between two infinities the perfect perspective of Dante, the sensorial mathematics of Novalis, the foundational hurricanes of Shakespeare, and the luminous shadows of Sade.

But just as language can be a fertilizing tide, it can also deteriorate into a stagnant pool that runs the risk of being overrun by the worst kinds of pollution. This can be seen in the effect Nazism had on the German language and in the systematic adulteration that fifty years of state socialism have imposed on the tongues of Central Europe. Even in these extreme cases, the danger is that the change does not take place in a day. The exchanges of meaning slow imperceptibly, and phrases and words grow heavier and heavier before they petrify into stereotypes. For want of being caught in the movement of new life, borrowed words remain foreign bodies. Because nothing is invented, we make the best of salvaged fragments that render the language increasingly vague.

Thus, instead of aiding thought to evolve, this approximate language acts so strongly as a brake that it prevents thought from living and slowly asphyxiates it under the weight of the amorphous words with which it is increasingly encumbered.

With his "frozen words," Rabelais was imagining this kind of calamity. An excessive number of examples have since taught us to pinpoint their location in connection with precise historical circumstances and with zones that are more or less easy to locate. The novelty is that the language mutation occurring today seems to be a phenomenon that knows no limits, a phenomenon aggravated by the violence—inconceivable until a short while ago—of a reality so full of itself that it cannot be contested.

Marcuse provided an accurate analysis of how, when influenced by technology, language "becomes functional and rejects all nonconformist elements from the structure and movement of speech."[3] This results in an increased production of "ritualized concepts" whose essential characteristic is to be "immune to contradiction."[4] From *free enterprise* to *surgical strikes,* or from the *clean bomb* to the *legal instrument,* the passage of time has unfortunately provided only further confirmation of this analysis.

This confirmation has attained such heights that a decisive line has been crossed, changing everything. While it is still possible to find someone to point out the formal contradiction of these "ritualized" formulas, the deplorable fact remains that nobody has truly questioned the consequences of their growing success since the early 1980s: namely, the strange manner in which the very idea of contradiction has simply disappeared behind its name. This is something people definitely refrain from mentioning, even though—as anybody can acknowledge—it is confirmed each day by those televised debates that are contradictory only in name. Even more striking in this regard is the recent beatification of Jean-Paul Sartre, whose philosophical contribution, if we are to take the word of Bernard-Henri Lévy, an expert in this kind of dodge, was that he blurred all difference between freedom and servitude, which squares completely with the advent of this consensual contradiction.

Today, in fact, all people are permitted—without it being at all shocking—to call themselves enemies of nationalism while at the same time they participate feverishly in the strong-armed cretinization of intrusive patriotism that is a necessary accompaniment to any sports competition. We will not soon forget the flood of insanities prompted at the 2005 World Cup; or those who played free spirits as they added their voices to the chorus of the most abject forms of morality (how much we have heard about the pedophilia that has suddenly been rediscovered at the end of the millennium!); or those claiming to be open to the riches of multiculturalism as they look to Interpol or the FBI to solve the problem of "illegal immigrants."

In noting these contradictions, we can also mark how unseemly if not old-fashioned it appears to recall the accusation of *incompatibility,* which was formerly an inescapable aspect of the term *contradiction* before this term became a synonym for *juxtaposition.* But it seems essential to draw attention to the inevitable reduction of meaning that has led gradually to a change of meaning—which has led to today's world that, far from being threatened by this new form of *contradiction,* seeks only its proliferation, as much for the purpose of avoiding any confrontations as for installing the most alarming kind of uniformity under the appearance of plurality.

This is no longer a matter of the cultivated caricature of dialectic, which Marcuse singled out as one of the ruses used by technological logic to further its own eye-deceiving perspective. We are far past this game with mirrors when the word, turned upside down in this way, seems to have no other destiny than to play the role of false witness under the pressure of a reality that remodels language as it pleases. This is the long-term effect of the reduction of language to a mere function. This reduction will prompt ever-greater changes that consequently cause us to unlearn our ability to discern by taking away our ability to feel.

8

A LANGUAGE OF SYNTHESIS

There has been a great deal of alarm over these last few years regarding the quality, or more exactly the harmful qualities, of what we eat. As the endless list of food contaminants has been revealed, the files on them cannot be closed again; they remain ajar permanently. Nevertheless, the mere mention of this phenomenon has produced a bizarre sense of satisfaction: While the problem has certainly not disappeared, we have been given the illusion that the most harmful effects have been neutralized. This is surely related to the fact that years of adulterated, reconstituted, and improperly altered foods have accustomed us to tasting the name of the food more than the food itself.

We have only to stroll through the aisles of any supermarket to appreciate the gastronomical rhetoric that now accompanies all products of the food industry. Such rhetoric has become an indispensable food additive in the same way that commentary on literary matters tends to take on more importance than the text it accompanies. Today, more than ever, no matter how much it may offend great minds, what happens in agriculture happens in culture, as Sade foresaw so clearly some two centuries ago: "All intellectual notions are so dependent upon the physical laws of nature that any comparisons provided us by agriculture will never be morally in error."

Thus, we may view literary phenomena—such as a Marcel Proust Garden project "in which there are life-sized constructions of things mentioned in *Remembrance of Things Past*";[1] the fantastic expression of Créolité* that was first manufactured on the model of the South American novel, then retailored to Parisian standards; and the countless "reinterpretations" of classic theater, which have replaced directing—a parallel to jams containing no fruit, fish meal, imitation crabmeat, and so on. But what is especially salient in both the cultural and alimentary realms is that the only purpose served by a name is to make up for the absence of what it is supposed to designate.

Daniel Mesguich† provided one example among many during the winter of 1995. His adaptation of Shakespeare's *Titus Andronicus,* with its large number of passages from other Shakespeare plays, as well as many borrowed from twentieth-century authors,§ did not leave much room for the original text. This is an aspect that the highly laudatory critics were, of course, in no position to notice. Recognizing these borrowings required a knowledge of the original literature. But this is not the worst part: Because the title had more importance than the play itself, what did the audience see but an appellation so well controlled that it was beyond any control?

This is not the least of the paradoxes that loom during the operation to subvert language: In this operation, the word itself is reduced to hoodwinking us as to the actual nature of the reality overload, while

*[Créolité is a French-Caribbean literary movement that originated in Martinique in the 1980s. —*Ed.*]

†[Daniel Mesguich is a French actor and director born in Algiers (1952). Films released in the United States in which he has appeared include *Le Divorce, The Musketeer, Jefferson in Paris,* and *The Rashevski Tango.* As a director, his work is influenced by the theories of Lacan and Derrida. His intention for *Titus Andronicus* (in bona fide French Theory terminology) was to force the audience to recognize the ontological instability of Shakespearean meanings, thus pointing to the absence of the original Author and the presence of the Director as the de facto Author. This destabilization of the performance was meant to destabilize the subject and explore theater's power to communicate. —*Trans.*]

§I first heard lines from Kafka, whom I recognized. Then, on two separate occasions, I could hardly believe my ears when I heard lines in the play that I had written a short time before on Sade.

at the same time the word is acknowledged to possess a new power through this *supremacy of appellation.*

Equally paradoxical is the fact that words went down lock, stock, and barrel during this operation to subvert language—as if their impact was greater in proportion to the degree to which they abandoned sensorial connections.

This breakdown has gone so far that even in the most common interactions, it now seems mandatory for all salient features of our inner life to be formulated in pseudoscientific jargon. For example, it is impossible to confide anything about our love life without using a host of intermingling words and expressions that have been borrowed indiscriminately from the social and human sciences. Hence the great confusion that arises when words such as *motivation, control, fantasy, validation, relationship, connection, mobilization, negotiation, demand, undertaking, fixation, projection, communication,* and so on, used here, there, and everywhere, are introduced into the personal sphere, as well as in psychoanalysis, psychology, sociology, history, and economics. The resulting mess devalues even the slightest sensorial expression—and such expressions are inevitably made destitute by the trashy objectivity of a language whose flaunted neutrality and technicality work toward the complete erasure of anything singular that an individual may still possess.

How are we to recognize Rimbaud's "young lovers" once they are turned into *sex partners* in the swarm of *relationships with others* about which everyone now speaks as if he or she was a specialist? If at times we deem it still worthwhile to recall that subjectivity is neither quantifiable nor measurable, we still have no escape from the words of the experts, each word as unfit for consumption as the next. We can only emphasize the vulgarity of the instrument that this falsely objective language forms in order to explain sensorial life. As we noted earlier, bioethics has a predilection for "the language of management," which engenders "a climate of cold psychosis like a symbolic breakdown,"[2] and this now holds true for the whole of inner life.

In fact, the inadequacy of this pseudoscientific language, with respect to the object it purports to describe, is comparable to the growing recourse to psychotropic medications for the indiscriminate treatment of psychoses, neuroses, phobias, anxieties, and depression. The effects of these medications are similar to those of anesthesia, denying the complexity of inner life and inducing a numbness that is well on its way to becoming the norm. We need only a modicum of awareness to assess the extent to which this gradual victory of exterior language over the inner life corresponds to a reality that crushes anything that does not serve its own expansion. This invasion of the inner world by an outside force intrinsically opposed to it has taken on catastrophic proportions. Why should we not see this as the equivalent of an oil spill? The only difference is that no one is volunteering to clean up the damage done to the beaches of language.

What is gained in irresponsibility is matched by a corresponding loss of discernment. Evidence of this loss is an immoderate recourse to euphemism aggravated by a use of acronyms that now smacks of an endemic phenomenon.

This is not to say that simple denial of the way things actually are has disappeared. Instead, it has simply taken a new turn by designating those circumstances that cannot be changed with euphemisms, such as *hearing challenged* for deaf. Similarly, the blind are now *sight challenged* and atheists are *belief challenged*. But the real novelty lies in the fact that over the course of the past ten years, this use of euphemism appears to have been unequal to the task assigned to it and has now been completely neutralized in the form of the acronym. The issue is no longer what cannot be changed but rather what should not be changed.

No doubt, resorting to acronyms is an old practice. It is not by chance that, from the CIA and the DST* to the FBI and the KGB, all the police forces of the world have resorted instinctively to the abstract

*[*Direction de la surveillance de la territoire* (Directorate of Territorial Surveillance): France's domestic intelligence agency. —*Trans.*]

neutrality provided by acronyms in order to conceal their dirty work. The prize, however, goes to the socialist regimes for the innovation of systematically joining acronym and denial—for there is nothing superior to the apparent objectivity of the acronym in both imposing and institutionalizing this denial by making it possible for us to overlook its outrageousness. For example, we see the word *democratic* appearing in the German Democratic Republic (GDR); and in the Union of Socialist Soviet Republics (USSR) we find the word *soviet,* which evokes the workers councils that were annihilated almost directly after the founding of the nation. These are examples that are now classic but are at odds with the current recourse to acronyms, whose essential goal is seemingly the avoidance of any mention of troubling realities—especially those that are sometimes capable of sparking revolt.

It is surely not out of modesty that *sexually transmitted diseases* exist now only as STDs. Similarly, it is not out of simple discretion that *nongovernmental organizations* are cited as NGOs. On its own, the mention of either of these terms, although somewhat ameliorated by the euphemism of the chosen formulation, continues implicitly to denounce the shortcomings and lies of a society claiming to be simultaneously liberal, hygienic, and humanitarian. This is certainly the reason it became urgent to resort to the anesthetizing qualities of the acronym. Further encouragement for proceeding on this path was the opportunity to confuse NGOs with GMOs (genetically modified organisms), the noble image of the former having a corrective influence on the dubious impression we might have of the latter. And there is no doubt that the objective behind the invention of *person of no fixed domicile,* which has metamorphosed today into SDF [*sans domicile fixe*], is to conceal beneath the fog of another category the growing number of those whom this world, so lavish with its social proclamations, forces into poverty before condemning to complete exclusion.

Thus, without anyone being aware of it, the individual disappears little by little in this new use of acronyms, which now refer only to qualities or, rather, to an absence of qualities. The major advantage of this way of speaking is that it conceals its content to such a degree that what the euphemism used to say becomes totally erased.

Consequently, it appears highly significant that the all-news television station LCI repeats its slogan every half hour—"LCI, all the news in three letters"—while an indiscriminate assortment of acronyms flow by on the screen: IGS, HLM, IMF, KGB, RPR, VIP, UNO, GNP, IRA, CGS, TGV, RTA, VAT. . . . This prepares us to accept with the same indifference AIH, AMP, IVG, OPA, and so on, which now form part of our lives in the same way as CD, DVD, and CDD.*

In order to subvert language completely, it has also been necessary to rob it, reducing it to nothing more than a flow of signs devoid of any presence. Its daily use, however, models a disappearance of the body coupled with the destruction of the negative. In this regard, the uninventive, backwards slang† that has become popular with adolescents in the last decade is the equivalent of a derisory depiction: We see not an upside down world, but the backside of a world that is reduced to exhibiting its inability to go beyond the most formal negations.

---

*[I have replaced some of these acronyms with those familiar to English speakers. A list of the others follows, along with the full French name of each and a brief description in English. —*Trans.*]

IGS = Inspection générale des services (equivalent to Metro Police)
HLM = Habitation à loyer modéré (low-income housing)
RPR = Rassemblement pour la République (a right-wing political party)
CGS = centimètre, gramme, seconde (units of measure)
TGV = Train à grande vitesse (French bullet train)
RTA = Régiment de Tirailleurs Algériens (Algerian Infantry Regiment)
AMP = Assistance médicale à la procréation (Medical Aid for Procreation)
IVG = Interuption voluntaire de grossesse (abortion)
OPA = Offre public d'achat (public offer to buy—i.e., a business takeover)
CDD = contrat a durée déterminée (contract for a predetermined period of time)

†[This slang, called *verlan* (the inversion of the two syllables making up the French term *l'envers,* meaning "backwards," "inside out," "upside down," and so on), involves the reversal of syllables. To use one of the better-known examples, *les pourri* (used to describe corrupt cops) becomes *les ripou*. Others are *chrome* for *moche* (ugly), *meuf* for *femme* (woman), and *laisse béton* for *laisse tomber* (forget about it). —*Trans.*]

■

At this juncture, it seems difficult to avoid a question posed by André Breton in 1924: "Doesn't the mediocrity of our world essentially depend on our power of enunciation?" Today "our "power of enunciation" is precisely the prey of this subverted language, whose grip grows stronger daily.

This seems especially true when we observe the increasingly frequent custom of accompanying the actions of modern life with derisory commentary (a custom that takes on familiar proportions with the cell phone); advertising, which supposedly plays exclusively on the image, relying more and more on word games; and the placing and replacing into verbal circulation of invented values such as *humanitarianism* and *dialogue,* as well as those now fallen into disuse, such as *patriotism* and *citizenship.* It thus becomes quite difficult to deny the sudden importance passed on to words, whose imminent demise has been announced to us rather than granting them any kind of credit. Of course, we should remember that these are no longer the same words. Forced, doped, conned, they no longer have even the need to draw their energy from what lives. That they exist only artificially in the closed circuit of words referring to words renders them all the more adaptable to our "networked" societies. They could even be considered the essential complement of these societies. It is as if in order to develop, the reality overload requires this proliferation of words that amounts to a *synthetic language.*

More precisely, this synthetic language is manufactured to eliminate, as we have seen, the portion of night that certain words can still transport as contraband. A share of this incommunicability allows others to disconnect from what has been programmed. This is the reason for the direct function of this synthetic language. Like user instructions diffused continuously as subtitles, it tells us what we should think and feel. "Politically correct" ideology, in which all reflection is replaced by conditioned reflexes that respond to an assembly of predetermined words, could certainly be one of its emanations.

The advent of this synthetic language corresponds to a sinister victory. Not only is this a victory of technological rationalism and its plan for total mastery over the unpredictable freedom that, in every language, invents itself to reinterpret the world, but also—more seriously—this victory is one of an infinitely open network, and, by virtue of this, naturally incompatible with the closed logic of any computer network. What we thought was our language is now the object of all speculation.

Furthermore, as the peerless rival of all other possible and imaginable networks—because of its subtlety and limitless wealth—it must be modified, and be able to survive only when it has been completely subverted. In other words, synthetic language can survive only when it has been completely reconstituted to prevent us from catching sight of the mutations to which it subjects us. This is done in such a way that the triumph of this synthetic language is also a triumph of a representation of the world that is manufactured again and again to compel our increased conformity to what we are less and less capable of challenging.

The proof that some are actively toiling toward this end can be found in a novelty of our time that consists of a pollution of space by text. This is created by the countless advertising banners that now mark our lives, and by highway billboards announcing the sites that no one visits anymore and the towns through which no one travels. What we have here is a new mode of debraining that invites all of us to exchange our simplest liberties—including the liberty to "traverse ideas like countries and cities," advocated by Picabia*—for the bombastic slogans that carve up space like rhetorical subdivisions.

And from one debraining method to another, these serve as similar pretexts "to talk a lot of fine words" about the "nonplaces" that Marc Augé views as the constituent elements of our "postmodernism." Now a fact of life, these elements cover "the necessary installations for the accelerated circulation of people and goods (rapid transit systems, highway interchanges, airports), as well as the means of transportation

*[Francis Picabia (1879–1953), avant-garde poet and painter of Franco-Spanish-Cuban origin, who was active in both Dada and the surrealist movement. —*Trans.*]

themselves, the great commercial centers, and even the transit camps in which the world's refugees are packed."[3]

By itself, the vogue for the term *space,* which now embellishes these "nonplaces" systematically, speaks of their emptiness, but also masks it by adding adjectives capable of evoking just what is lacking: *freedom, recreation, luxury, pleasure. . . .* How many "beauty spaces," "health spaces," "leisure spaces," and "free spaces" have overrun us in recent years, like so many cages whose charms are offered to us in closed circuits? How many similar examples exist in which the reality overload also exercises its unstoppable brutality, using language to disguise the fact that this plethora of "spaces," whose existence is circumscribed by their names, constitutes the best means of destroying the very notion of space and its indeterminate, freedom-bearing nature?

At this point, we may note to what extent the fate of language determines the fate of space. In fact, it is the symbolic use of both that is threatened in the same way. This division of space into equal "spaces" is enough to ensure that, fooled by the illusory difference of their names, we find ourselves dispossessed of a wealth of meaning without which there is quite simply no longer enough space for infinity to open to us its "lyrical prairies."

We are thus compelled to admit that this subversion of language brings about a generalized demetaphorization, which blocks every exit. However, its new strength lies in its ability to disguise this state of affairs beneath the lie of an aestheticizing realism. In fact, even if none of these free spaces takes anyone anywhere, no one has perceived a closing device hidden skillfully there by design—a design that consists of its translation into a plastic means of expression and consequently repeats what its name allegedly means.

The misfortune is that there is no difference among the artistic, literary, and political cages, which suggests that all people should exercise their talents on condition—above all else—of trying not to escape. And if our time has every reason to congratulate itself on this, then it is further evidence of today's allegiance to the reality overload. Because people lack the inner strength to go elsewhere, they now display a concern only to revisit what already exists. But they do this with an imposed arrogance that is the surest means of hiding the fact that all their energy is spent in this territorial refurbishing.

It is as if they find themselves already beyond demetaphorization. Under pretext of creation, the impossibility of the metaphorical transport is established everywhere. We can discern this in the calamitous "get-away places" and "leisure spaces." Thus, it is all the more interesting to consider how some of this world's spokespeople have recently deemed it useful to invoke a metaphor that has never been more off the mark.

9

WHERE IS THE METAPHOR?

We can recall the stir caused by the two scientists Alan Sokal and Jean Bricmont. Sokal had already ruffled feathers when, with a successful hoax, he cast ridicule on the editors of the prestigious journal *Social Text,* a bastion of deconstructionism in the United States. Then, Sokal and Bricmont together exhibited the poor taste to list what the philosophers, psychoanalysts, and theoreticians in vogue—from Jacques Lacan and Julia Kristeva to Luce Irigaray, Paul Virilio, and Jean Baudrillard—had deemed worthy enough to extract from mathematics and physics.*

Perhaps the in-vogue thinkers had searched naively in the exact sciences for something that could bring more precision to the human sciences. Unfortunately, the examples amassed by Sokal and Bricmont illustrate instead that these philosophers, psychoanalysts, and theoreticians had a complete incomprehension of the original material they used. Unfortunately, it was not realized that no one was in a position to contest this.

*[Alan Sokal submitted a paper with made-up jargon to *Social Text* to see if the prestigious journal would, as "A Physicist Experiments with Cultural Studies," in *Lingua Franca,* quotes Sokal, "publish an article liberally salted with nonsense if (a) it sounded good and (b) it flattered the editors' ideological preconceptions." Bricmont and Sokal are coauthors of the book *Fashionable Nonsense,* which exposes the abuses and referential errors of scientific concepts in the works of many postmodern theoreticians and thinkers. —*Ed.*]

The most extraordinary aspect of the Sokal and Bricmont affair, however, was that the controversy never centered on those who were implicated. No doubt, they could have been fairer-minded and behaved less like formalist heirs to the Age of Enlightenment, but of the thousand and one critics who targeted Sokal and Bricmont, none refuted any of the listed thinkers' erroneous and capricious uses of scientific data. There seemed to be an implicit acceptance of the incriminating borrowing—and critics seemed to have the notion that it was unseemly to speak of the borrowers.

In this silence there flourished the combination of nonsense and craftiness. Then Julia Kristeva shoved her way to the front of the line—and she seemed to confuse questioning of her methods with an insult made, in her words, "through me against the whole of France."[1] All it took, in fact, was two foreign scientists—an American and a Belgian—to expose the type of opening bluff she used to cobble together her useless literary theory. The result: She immediately shouted "Francophobia!" and depicted this criticism as nothing less than the sign of "a new division of the world, pitting ravenous interests against the inner reaches of identity."[2]

Yet lingering in the putrid morass of this deeply entrenched line of reasoning was soon seen as too risky. The solution: Move from the notion of threatened France to the notion of the threatened metaphor. The observations of the two scientists would be countered in the name of poetry. With this tactic, all could be saved. Julia Kristeva even explained—doubtless to anyone who has read her pompous, heavy prose—that in the human sciences, "reflection is closer to poetic metaphor than to modeling."[3] With this, Sokal and Bricmont became thick-skulled rationalists who were incapable of understanding the work of a thought in search of itself. The proof was that they saw only fraud where there was metaphorical usage of obviously scientific ideas—and these ideas were themselves borrowed from the common tongue.

■

This argument could have carried some weight if it had not been founded on a bizarre conception of metaphor. Instead, to further the cause, it was transformed into a large rattletrap, a bus capable of carrying anything. It became contrary to the very definition of metaphor, which is a transport inseparable from the means of transportation—a precise means of successfully transferring meaning between two objects that, at first glance, appear to have no connection. With successful metaphor, it is necessary to have a perfect grasp of the nature of these two objects in order to find their tangential point—the only point from which the analogical connection emerges, like a beam of light, to illuminate the objects with an utterly new perspective.

If such illumination does not occur, it is wrong-headed to speak of metaphor at all. This is even more clear when we "import" from another discipline technical terms, key concepts, and formulas, which can be lifeless and meaningless when taken out of their usual context. Referring to *black holes* and *chaos*—physicists' terms borrowed from common language and having meanings that everyone can grasp—is not at all the same as invoking Gödel's theory or the *commutable operators,* whose use in ordinary prose only intimidates. What's more, the importers of such terms seem to have no better grasp of their primary meaning than any other Tom, Dick, or Harry.

In fact, this kind of approximation is completely antithetical to metaphor, which stipulates that we must understand profoundly the two objects being compared in order for one object to be lit from within by our rediscovering it through the comparison. Without this dazzling effect it has upon us to carry us to what had previously been overshadowed by either object, there is no metaphor.

We must concede that this does not occur in any of Sokal's and Bricmont's examples—the scientific references they cite only lend greater obscurity to texts that are already dark enough on their own. And how could it be otherwise, with authors undoubtedly in agreement with

Julia Kristeva,* seeing "metaphoricity"—to which they have profitably devoted themselves—as "the indication of an uncertainty with respect to the reference"?[4]

"*Being like* is not simply *being* and *non-being;* it is also an aspiration to *unbeing* in order to affirm as the sole possible *being* not an ontology—that is to say, something exterior to discourse—but the constraint of discourse itself."[5] For once, the obscurity is extremely transparent: No light can be expected from a discourse that, for lack of any roots in the senses, goes so far as to confess its creation by "the constraint of discourse itself." Finally, thank goodness, Baudelaire can explain to us Julia Kristeva's almost magical recourse to metaphor when she compares criticism of herself to criticism of France: "Every metaphor here wears a mustache."

At this point, we may ask ourselves which is more troubling: the vile enormity of the mistaken notion of metaphor or the scientific mystification it camouflaged? This is an especially apt question, given that, behind this mystification, we cannot miss a demented desire for control that aims at a limitless expansion of the rational field. Further, this occurs at a time when true science is questioning its own possible applications as well as its very foundations. The frenzied unanimity with which the borrowers and their numerous defenders have started brandishing the absolute weapon—a metaphor is not a metaphor—is even more alarming because in this brandishing, these borrowers and

*I noted several years earlier, in a text entitled *Du kitsch théorique de Julia Kristeva* [On the Theoretical Kitsch of Julia Kristeva], that Kristeva had no need of science to cast darkness everywhere, when she showed us the realm of the "invisible metaphor" with regard to Baudelaire. She accomplished this under the pretext that "[i]f there is a mysticism or mystery in Baudelaire, this is where it resides: in the possibility for that superannuated self to *call* itself metaphorically 'vaporized' due to the contract upheld with the other. Through this broadened metaphoricity, it embraces the entire spectrum of psychism and substitutes itself for the primal repression." See *Histoires d'amour* [Love Stories] (Paris: Gallimard, 1983), 407, cited in *À distance* (Paris: Jean-Jacques Pauvert/Carrère, 1984), 216.

defenders are proclaiming the excellence of something precisely while they are working hard to annihilate it.

This nonexistence of metaphor is emblematic of the current situation as a whole. For example, many professor-theoreticians, greedy to extend the realm of their expertise and their power, show us that a kind of rational violence now threatens all sensorial expression. The current situation also demonstrates that to exercise any kind of intellectual or artistic power, it is no longer enough to deny what *is;* those who would be powerful must assert the existence of what others have tried to make disappear in order to cover the ravages caused by the reality overload. We can only be struck by the remarkable progress of a process that is now sophisticated enough to produce, on demand, the most virtual of positivities.

We might say that this progress is fairly minor during a time when we are perpetually drilled on the advent of "virtual reality." Here again, it and its accompanying jury-rigged metaphysic mask rather than illustrate the gravity of the situation. This swindling by metaphor has not shocked very many people, although fundamentally it is just as scandalous as the erroneous use of scientific references (which started this whole affair). Furthermore, the general agreement on this point by the entire dominant intellectual class speaks volumes about the state of this class. Therefore, we can only praise the remark made by Jacques Bouveresse: "In this kind of debate, the use made of the notion of the poetic metaphor as something always available to justify or excuse almost anything seems to me an insult to real poetry."[6] With this comment, the silence of those who call themselves poets weighs even heavier. Such a subversion of the notion of metaphor cannot be a matter of indifference to them. Could it be that their existence is just as fictitious as that of the all-purpose metaphor?

Unfortunately, these poets give us no reason to think otherwise. The overwhelming majority of them have tolerated the "necessary" caricature of the metaphor in order to serve in such a wretched argument.

Likewise, they have tolerated the denial of the metaphor's evocative power in order to assist hollow discourses. All is explained, however, in the works of these alleged poets. It is enough to read the samples of their poetry as regularly served up to us by critics who are ready to swallow anything in order to avoid being castigated like their predecessors for having systematically missed what truly mattered. It nevertheless remains difficult to imagine anything more rancid than the anthologies* in which known and unknown names (for each seasonal delivery must also be the object of a revelation) compete in affectation to open over the same void. Miserable textual games and wheezy simulations of impulse-driven writing are manufactured to illustrate theories that have been sterile for thirty years. Some poems celebrate breathlessly life's emptiest moments or present the worst platitudes, formulated preciously in order to lend them a metaphysical air. Finally, such writings concoct sentimental considerations or a particularly indigent prose that is birthed into poetic existence through the audacity of starting a new paragraph.

Therefore, we cannot be surprised that these specialists in confining language have not defended a metaphor, which, by analogy, puts the body back into language. Why would they expend any energy to protect what they are fighting? We have almost reached the point of pining for those "large soft heads" reviled by Lautréamont when we see that our own era presents us with this collection of pinheads whose skin changes are dictated solely by the tics and tackiness that determine their cultural cages.

But we should not confuse the *fin de siècle*—the end of the twentieth century—with the end of the nineteenth century, during which nei-

*I have before me an anthology that *Le Monde* served up to its readers on August 15, 1998: *Poésies vivantes d'aujourd'hui* [Living Poems of Today]. To use Alfred Jarry's expression, the title "says it all." Although I missed out on the harvest of 1999, the subsequent crops of analogies that have accompanied each "Springtime of Poetry" have done nothing to change my point of view.

ther writing nor commitment was a going concern. Rather, the end of the nineteenth century witnessed far better adventures enriched by the meeting of and profound sympathies between, for example, the Symbolists and the Anarchists. "They were symbolist in literature and anarchist in politics. Stéphane Mallarmé, Remy de Gourmont, Francis Vielé-Griffin, Pierre Quillard, and Saint-Pol Roux all left evidence to confirm this."[7] In 1893, Remy de Gourmont remarked that the decadents could "accept only one form of government: the anarchy,"[8] and stated, even more explicitly, that symbolism, "washed of the offensive signifiers given it by short-sighted cripples, is literally translated by the word *liberty* and, for the violent, by the word *anarchy*."[9] It was thus completely natural for Mallarmé to testify at the trial of Félix Fénéon and contribute to Francis Vielé-Griffin's review *Les Entretiens politiques et littéraires* (Political and Literary Discussions), whose anarchist orientation was never in doubt. Likewise, Émile Verhaeren and Saint-Pol Roux were contributors to Zo d'Axa's *L'Endehors* (The Outsider), "which in the first six months of 1892 earned its founder seven years and four months of prison and 13,150 francs in fines."[10] And we can add to this example that of Marcel Schwob, or Jarry "he who revolvers"? What about Louise Michel, who in 1886 publicly stood up for the decadents: "Our senses are still imperfect but the thought of man can take on any sound, any harmony, any form. . . . The anarchists, like the decadents, wish for the annihilation of the old world. The decadents are creating the anarchy of style."[11]

The end of the nineteenth century was a time in which poetry was quite naturally involved with revolt. Is it so strange that poetry comports itself best during those moments when life returns through it to shatter the cages of genres, roles, and customs?

PART TWO

10

POETIC OUTRAGEOUSNESS

"It has been estimated that more than fifty million individuals have lost their lives to wars and religious massacres. Is there even one among them worth the blood of a single bird?" This vision of Sade's evokes best what we may still expect of poetry in these destitute times—or, to be more exact, what we may expect of *poetic outrageousness.* Here, in all the excess and insult that lead us suddenly to consider with a single glance the immense plains of crime, we witness the brusque unveiling of the falsehoods of those partial views that we habitually cling to, in order to condemn certain extortions but above all to justify others.

By at first savagely negating everything that so-called poetry (which perpetually justifies and embalms the status quo) is striving to achieve, Sade's viewpoint strikes us like lightning, and opens our hearts at a new perspective the greatest possible distance from who we think we are. Sade's invitation to contemplate such fleeting perspectives on the suddenly inverted horizon of importance allows us to ask what remains of the rationalist foundations we thoughtlessly ascribe to tolerance, humanism, and ecology.

Yet the reversal of a point of view cannot, on its own, explain the rerouting of certainties we witness. We see the spectacle of life disarming every claim we possess in order to manage it. When Apollinaire writes to his young lover, Lou, "The mare's vulva is pink like yours," or when Novalis declares, "The organs of thought are the genitals of nature," the unprecedented splendor of the reprobate both dumbfounds and liberates us.

Moreover, this poetic outrageousness is so foreign to any notion of beauty, taste, or talent that it dissuades us from measuring any contemporary poet on his or her own merits. Yet, though it manifests in the most diverse ways—like a rocket with Apollinaire, like sudden gusts with Jarry, like a whirlwind with Sade—it is always aimed at tearing beings and objects and ideas from the interwoven ideological, moral, and sentimental considerations with which we hobble them.

We can never say too many times what we owe this violence, which, for a moment, allows us to win by losing—as if by enchantment—the ideas with which we stubbornly adorn the nothingness over which we advance. We see this in the incredible tenderness of the skin of women who, Germain Nouveau swears to us, are nourished on the "brains of boxers," and in the murderous arrival of Ubu* on the symbolic stage, and in Apollinaire's proclaimation:

I do not sing this world or the other stars
I sing all the possibilities of myself
beyond this world and stars . . .

We surely find it in Jarry's assuring us: "The act of love is of no importance, in that it can be performed indefinitely."

It is this poetic outrageousness that can still give us the measure of infinite freedom. We can also speculate that the specific purpose behind the current promotion of uplifting poetry is to make us forget the uncontrollable power of rupture—a power that rips apart the mesh of our customary ways of seeing and cuts our moorings. We, in our weakness, find these wretched images of ourselves satisfactory. In fact, there is no longer any threat to some people's conception of the world's

*[Ubu is the main character in three Alfred Jarry plays (*King Ubu, Ubu Cuckolded,* and *Ubu Enchained*) that satirize European philosophies. —*Ed.*]

order, especially at a time when the reference to "networks," prevalent in every realm, is the sign of a continuous closing of reality upon itself. In the past several years, there has even been talk of a "network philosophy" that would be "our new mirror."[1]

Now, nothing is more normal than the sight of poetry's new promoters joining forces with its declared enemies—the Kundera* variety, followed by several minuscule hussars. This conceals the real stakes, for both sides have an equal interest in denying the thing that resists being monopolized: that quality, which presents a continuous threat to tear us from ourselves through poetic outrageousness. Whether it be, according to Lautréamont, to "stop on the road for a moment in the way one looks at a woman's vagina" or, as Sade expresses, "one day, on contemplating Etna whose heart was vomiting flames," to simply desire "to be that famous volcano."

What our artificial poets today dread is precisely this way of having done with everything that seems self-evident. This is also dreaded by the partisans of the novel, which is pitted against poetry, especially in justification of the major and minor compromises that have been made with the world. It is not the wretched headline-making efforts of our current poets that are capable of alarming these defenders of fictional realism. Just as respectful of the status quo as of the litany of the alleged poets whose kitsch they denounce, these novel partisans are fearful of the long-range negation. Through poetic outrageousness, true poets threaten the very foundations of a representation that is capable of congealing what it claims to depict.

---

*[Milan Kundera, a Czech-born novelist who has lived in exile in France since 1975, was blacklisted in his native country for his criticism of the Soviet invasion. What the author is referring to here is Kundera's stated opinion that lyrical poetry is essentially responsible for the gulag; his contention is weakened by his attempt to hold up Breton as an example by ascribing to him the responsibility for the hanging of a former Czech surrealist supporter by the Communist government, whereas it was the former surrealist poet, Paul Eluard, who had become an official Stalinist poet, who refused to use his considerable influence to ask for a pardon for the life of Zavis Kalandra. —*Trans.*]

Though the poets and the novelists use contrary methods, both take to heart conformity to the reality overload. It is downright disconcerting to see them killing themselves trying to create *the* aesthetic substance intended to conceal everything that doesn't bow to the order of things. This is how, over the last several years, poetry has become prosified and the novel has become poeticized. All we have to do is read the few lines of Bernard Noël's poem "Forbach," which has recently been posted in Metro cars, to learn that winter in the north is cold, the toil of workers is hard, and life is short. But I will let readers who have not been lucky enough to ride in the right car decide for themselves:

Partout les temples de la vielle misère
Maisons de peine et d'attente et de trop peu
Être humain est un long travail d'illusion
La neige et le froid un bien petit hiver
*À côté des exigences de l'espoir.**

On the fictional front, Philippe Sollers owes his latest success to a prose in which disjointed and pusillanimous erotico-touristic impressions, embellished by half again as many quotations, finds its common thread in a short-winded sentimentality for easily exhausted Club Med members.

Thus it matters little whether some base their efforts on sophistication or mawkish sentiment and others on *miserabilism*† or cynicism when everyone is motivated by the same goal of overburdening reality with its reflections, no matter what its colors. All that matters is the intensive production, whose effect is to erase the very existence of the

*[Temples of old poverty are everywhere
Houses of hardship and want and too little
To be human is a long effort of illusion
The snow and cold are a very short winter
Next to the unreasonable demands of hope. —*Trans.*]

†[*Miserabilism* is a word coined by André Breton to describe the offspring of the coupling of Stalinism and Hitlerite fascism and existentialism: "the depreciation of reality in place of its exaltation." —*Trans.*]

desire to shake things up—a desire that the great poets were sometimes capable of arousing and that gives us the possibility to be everything we are not. This is true whether we speak of Lautréamont ("It is a man or a stone or a tree who is going to begin the fourth canto") or Novalis, who declaims: "We are simultaneously inside nature and outside of her."

At the very moment when we find ourselves caught in the snare of a world that all now call "connectionist," we can recall both this mad desire to get away and the necessary lightning flashes accompanying it; all the more so when the generalization of "representation in networks"—on which philosophers, sociologists, and scientists are all in accord—would explain a novelty to which little attention has been paid, to wit, that in all domains the liquidation of the negative has been attained by the liquidation of distance.

In this sense, poetic outrageousness takes every opportunity to rekindle Lautréamont's inestimable recommendation that "[w]e must take the distance into account." Efforts are being made to abolish this distance around beings and things, as well as around ideas and sensations, under the pretext of communication. The truth of this can be judged by reading an edifying extract taken from the book by Pierre Lévy modestly titled *World philosophie:*

> The existence and densification of transportation and communication networks is manifested by a process of general interconnectedness that entails a shrinkage of the space of practical experience, and, at the same time, draws human beings together and enlarges their perspectives. This, in short, is the essence of the globalization process. Thus history truly does have a meaning.[2]

So now we know how the reality overload is getting the better of us—and how it is also gaining the upper hand over the level of thought created by this miraculous form of communication, which is poetic outrageousness, therefore preventing the conception, and even the perception, of any form of negation.

11

A NEW ORDER OF PROMISCUITY

In one of his conversations with Johann Eckermann, Goethe mentioned the young artists who were going to Rome more to parade in "their long locks, their mustaches, their collars turned over their old fashioned frock coats, their pipes, and their bulldogs" than to learn anything about Raphael, whom they thought "weak," or Titian, whom they regarded as "a good colorist, nothing more." Goethe concluded: "Niebuhr was right . . . when he foresaw a return to barbarism. It is already here; we are in the midst of it, for what is barbarism if not precisely the inability to recognize what is excellent?"[1]

Though nicely phrased, Goethe's conclusion still requires the existence of the possibility to achieve excellence. The last decade has shown that we are far from any such possibility. Oddly enough, this seems of little concern to the disapproving critics of a new barbarism, denigrators who should have no trouble reading signs of this barbarism in the disappearance of the subject, the weakening of political life, and the foundering of culture.

Yet while these critics often take the relay of a critique begun long ago by Horkheimer and Adorno, the majority of them recognizing the misdeeds of a reason given unlimited power, these same parties still looked to that same reason to further develop that critique. Their reliance on reason is so pronounced that there is something tragic in seeing them cling to conceptual and ethical frameworks that have already given way under the pressure of the reality overload.

For example, what point is there in appealing to the "transcendence of meaning" when language, as we have seen, conceals every kind of trafficking in meaning, including the whitewashing of ideas? In fact, this denunciation of the new barbarism—we have only to examine its origins and its effects—has become a kind of philosophical or literary genre encouraged by the media, as if the purpose of deploring such barbarism prevents any attempts to change it.

All things considered, it is much less disturbing to be unaware of what is excellent than not to be capable—like experts on barbarism—of assessing a situation in which excellence is impossible. In the best case, this is the sign of a blindness linked to the anachronism of continuing to refer to a hierarchy of values that is not necessarily antiquated, but no longer has any grasp of the world. This is a world whose symbolic forms are changing under the pressure of a reality that has almost succeeded in making us confuse the virtual and the imaginary.

In fact, we may ask what logic or transcendence we can claim when increasingly "the recourse to the notion of network results . . . from the ambition to suggest very general expressions and models capable of tying together all manner of individuals without necessarily specifying their nature, is treated as a property emerging from the network itself."[2]

Under these conditions, there is no longer any question of pitting the vertical nature of a hierarchy of values against the horizontal nature of a world developing as a network. By itself, the endurance (I won't go so far as to say "rigidity") of these values makes them inapplicable to a self-generating reality that proliferates by flow systems.

Accordingly, many great minds are legitimately shocked by the hodgepodges resulting from the worst cultural demagoguery (which urges us to see the future of painting in taggers* or puts rappers and

*[Graffiti artists. —*Ed.*]

countertenors on the same level). These great minds preach for the return of "true culture" and "great art." By not taking into consideration the major contribution made by a modernism that has long overturned the traditionalist aesthetic, these new destroyers of barbarism defend a beauty imprisoned by their rationalist conception of the world—a conception for which the neoculture they claim to be fighting (including the Internet) is one of the latest avatars. They fail to understand that the sole energy capable of opposing such barbarism still lives at the heart of a modernism that has opened the aesthetic domain to the tempests of the mind. Therefore, all they can do is run short of breath, playing war between the Old School and the Moderns, while the true battlefield lies elsewhere. The equivocal nature of these thinkers' combat is such that they are placed in the first rank of the specialists about whom our era is so keen. They are the benevolent suppliers of a critique always destined to miss its mark.

Because they never hit the target, some of these defenders of cultural tradition, to their credit, took up the cause at the time of the war in Kosovo against the Milosevic regime. It was no surprise that none of them mentioned the names Baudelaire and Rimbaud, which had been given at the beginning of the summer of 1999 to two French army units sent to help restore order in the region. It is as if the cultural box closes once the political box is opened, and vice versa. Could it be that Rimbaud and Baudelaire do not make up part of what these defenders of tradition consider to be true culture? Then again, perhaps these great minds are innately incapable of seeing the monstrosity of giving the names of these two rebellious individuals to any division of the army. It was Rimbaud, after all, who deserted the Dutch Foreign Legion and Baudelaire who declared he would never cease "to insult France"!

In any case, no one has found any fault with the frenetic promotion of poetry. Indeed, the Paris Metro became the terrain of choice a few years ago on the occasion of the first "Spring of the Poets"—an event signifying that we have reached a point of no return.*

The calamitous "Autumn of the Novelists" that has resulted shows that it is not at all a matter of setting fictional truth against poetic lies or realism against lyricism, as Philippe Muray appears to think. Today, novelists and poets are joined in the same abjection: The disposition of both parties to conform to the existing order cannot offset an equally shared lack of vision. When I wrote the above lines, I had not yet read page 157 and the following pages of this same book. In them Philippe Muray, thoroughly appalled by the "Amazing Traveler's Festival" in the town of Saint-Malo, which usually gave a warm welcome to novelists, realized that "[t]he haste with which I declared that the novel was incapable of being given its own festival needs to be corrected."

The defenders of tradition would have us believe that it is sacrilege to display a poem side by side with an advertisement. Yet we must leave these inconsolable mourners of academic culture to their belief in a higher art that has nothing whatsoever to do with everyday life and should not be subject to comparison to modes of popular expression, especially advertising. If any "failure of thought" is to be found here, its origin lies in the defense of this kind of hierarchy, which has been thoroughly demolished by everything that has illuminated sensorial life for more than a century. From the "idiot paintings" hailed by Rimbaud and the use of advertisements by the surrealists to Apollinaire and his collages of conversational fragments in *Lundi rue Christine* [Monday Christine Street] and the cubists with their inclusion of newspapers and packing material in their work, we know how much poetry is fed by the street. But we must not forget that what has been found must always

*[There is one recent exception. In his *Après l'histoire II* (After History, volume 2) (Paris: Les Belles Lettres, 2000), Philippe Muray speaks out against this mummery that was intended to begin anew every year with the "Spring of the Poets." Unfortunately, he was still overly optimistic when he stated his belief that a "Spring of the Novelists" was an impossibility. We need only see how these latter pursue the prizes of the rentrée every year. (*La rentrée* is the period following the annual summer vacation, a traditional time for publication of new books—especially those considered important.) —*Trans.*]

undergo a transmutation—even if only caused by being retired from circulation in order to acquire a totally different meaning in an entirely different space.

This space is imaginary, one that is constantly renewed with power and that becomes everyone's individual space by virtue of the fact that it overflows the typographical surface of the text or the surface of the painting. Yet all it takes to prevent the conquest of this imaginary perspective—the destination of all true poetic itineraries—is to circumscribe the text or the painting by assigning, as occurs today with poetry in the Metro, a place and strict meaning that are foreign to it. Therefore, if someone was looking for proof of barbarism, it would be not in the crushing of a hierarchy of ever contestable values, but rather in this framing, which is equivalent to a mutilation. Juxtaposition is a far cry from transmutation.

There are those, however, who try to convince us otherwise in order to win our acceptance of the new order of promiscuity upon which our reality overload is founded. It hardly matters if we achieve this vulgarly by slapping up one poem after another on the platforms of the Saint-Germain Metro station in a quantity proportional to the replacement of this quarter's bookstores by ready-to-wear boutiques. One of the most noteworthy consequences of this promiscuity is its paradoxical disservice to Baudelaire, author of *Les Fleurs du mal* [Flowers of Evil]. And thanks to this promiscuity, poems that are, at the least, unequal are posted next to one another on one of this Metro station's platforms: "Jeunesse" [Youth] by Andrée Chedid and "Parfum exotique" [Exotic Perfume] by Charles Baudelaire.

Like Baudelaire's "The Albatross," whose humiliation in the midst of "the crewmen" is shown by the poet, his "Parfum exotique" gives an impression of mutilation, condemned as it is to share the wall with Andrée Chedid's sentimental mediocrity. From the moment it was committed to the wall, there was no longer any room for "his giant wings." This is not to say that Baudelaire, "similar to the prince of clouds," would be here "exiled to the ground in the midst of the jeering crowd"—but this promiscuity, aggravated by the fact that Baudelaire is used as a security payment for the poetic abjection of Charlotte Delbo, Charles Le Goffic, André Fernaud, and Arlette Humbert-Laroche, who are pasted on the same Metro platform, is equally fatal to him. Here we find him, like the albatross, prevented from living in the space necessary for his wingspan, and, because of this, compelled to imitate those "great seabirds" who let "their great white wings drag piteously alongside them like oars." Finally, upon noting that the promotional slogan chosen for this poetry enterprise in the Metro is "La rime dans la rame,"* we find that our age of connoisseurs has no reason to envy the vulgarity and mockery inspired by the sailors' prisoner, Baudelaire's "winged traveler."

Baudelaire, who always knew just where he stood, once remarked: "If a poet asked the state for the right to keep some bourgeois in his stable, this would cause great astonishment, whereas if a bourgeois asked for some roast poet, this would be seen as completely natural." Well, we can now see the truth of this statement.

It should also be no surprise that the word *galvauder* (to sully), whose primary meaning is "to compromise through ill use," should have fallen out of favor, like so many other words that we use to describe this omnipresent and ongoing process. Simultaneously meaning "to demean," "to dishonor," "to waste," "to lose," "to debase," and "to degrade," it would be a great help to portray the true goal of these operations against poetry. One example of this portrayal can be found in the attempt of the Sonia Rykiel stores to win recognition throughout this vile Spring of the Poets. These stores were turned upside down by the half-price discount offered by this cultural policy: By placing the poems of André Breton and Pablo Neruda in close proximity on the floors of their display windows, they provided a prime exhibit of today's cultural obscen-

*[This is a play on words: *rime* means "rhyme" in French, and *rame* can mean "ream" and "subway," as well as "paddle." —*Trans.*]

ity. Rather than attempting to use poetry to sell cute sweaters for three hundred dollars apiece, this practice used the pretext of exalting woman to create a coexistence of Breton's true lyrical élan alongside the aesthetic counterfeit that Neruda resorted to in order to camouflage the law-and-order implications of his Stalinist servility.

The secret of this successful merging of poetry and merchandise is to banish all critical perspectives and suspend all judgment. In an era whose sole ambition is to accentuate the positive, it is as if poetry's role is to lay it on thick in the most trivial sense of the term, in order to prevent the slightest manifestation of the negative.

It was on the command of "Everybody Grab Your Pens!" that, in 1999, the instigators of the second "RATP* prize for poetry, with the complicity [sic] of Télérama," invited everyone to "get carried away by poetry." In addition, they indicated explicitly that the jury would be chaired by Pierre Perret.† "Things Go Better with Reading" was also the tag line of a "Télérama soirée placed under the auspicious star of poetry: meetings with poets, readings, and conversations. . . ." But since it is much more difficult to halt cultural progress than the other variety, the same newspaper ran the headline: "On the Road toward the Constellation of the Little Verse Writers."[3] These words could not have been more true: The newspaper presented the writers as plucked from the "circle of unknown poets": "the lyricism of everyday life." Here we found "a brilliant essayist, dashing professor, and tireless traveler," and even "a safe and sound rhymer" who "loves adventure but carves his verse at the kitchen table while wearing his slippers, lulled by the purr of the fridge." As for the negative, it was fruitless to search for even the slightest trace; negativity has never existed in the land of the "little verse writers."

Anyone who contemplates love and "its black enchantments" that

*[RATP: Régie autonome des transports parisiens (the Paris Metro and bus system). —*Ed.*]

†[Pierre Perret (b. 1934) is a French singer and composer who specializes in integrating colorful street slang into his work, which can range from typical love songs and even children's songs to political protests and smutty ballads. —*Trans.*]

haunt Baudelaire is a real troublemaker. And into the Dumpster with that "ivory-eyed, pale god of woe" about whom Apollinaire speaks. Never again should anyone read about the body that fascinated Rimbaud when "that entire body moves and extends its fat rump, hideously beautiful with an ulcer on her anus."

But poetry is not everything. The RATP, France Télévision, La Cinquième,* Radio France, Skyrock, *Le Monde,* Eurostar, and several intellectuals from the world of haute couture, sponsored under the leadership of Jack Lang† at the first Spring of Poetry, tell us so in the press packet for this "display of national scope." The goal of this display is to "promote poetry in all its forms and in every contemporary medium in order to shed full light on the new burst of a *happy, enthusiastic,* and *inventive* poetry§ for which rap, public readings, and film scenarios are emblematic today."

We can recall that the totalitarian systems of the twentieth century distinguished themselves by the same confirmed taste for a radiant culture of happiness. Stalin and Hitler were cheerful characters when it came to culture, and the trend continued until the regime of Tito, who, toward the end of his life, condemned everything that appeared too somber in order to promote—indeed, command—the creation of a "rosy" literature and music. Times have certainly changed: Poetry has become an antidepressant that we are obliged to swallow in the street, the subway, the rail stations, and the airports—all of which are becoming far too familiar dreamscapes.

This force-fed poetry—a French innovation—has everything going for it to seduce our era, and can work well beyond the French national borders. We did not have to wait long: As of January 2000, Paris was no longer in first place for this debraining through confusion. Los Angeles

*[French public television network. —*Ed.*]

†[French Socialist politician born in 1939. He was the former French Minister of Culture. —*Trans.*]

§These are my italics.

can now pride itself on the poetic billboards it has had erected, allegedly to break the monotony of its highways. The words of Shakespeare, Charles Bukowski, and Emily Dickinson are placed on the same level as those of Neruda and other salaried minstrels whose miserable verses are inserted in counterpoint to the others by the zapping of the advertisements to which our towns and countryside are now subject. There is no longer any good reason to go out in the "open air." Threatened like the ozone layer, it is in the process of disappearing catastrophically wherever we go. If this new mania for placing poetry within the reach of everyone has a single merit, it is that of revealing, beyond all doubt, the encircling maneuver with which interposed culture is targeting us—and through this, the reality overload engulfs everything that has so far escaped it.

Yet this occurs without anyone perceiving the extent to which this spectacular operation—in each case playing on the apparent exploitation of a poem, the end result being to neutralize it while transforming it into an interchangeable commodity—constitutes a model of an unprecedented interference. It is because of the unique characteristic of this cultural miracle to make things that are physically compatible into things that are fundamentally incompatible. It is a veritable formatting of the lyrical register. One day, it will be worth inquiring what role computer science has played in the instigation of this sensorial surveillance grid, which is far more sophisticated than what has been achieved through the idea of nuclear destruction. Through this sensorial surveillance, the conformist principle of a new kind of totalitarianism—one based on the establishment of pluralism without conflict and without end—is being implanted in the depths of our emotions.

The Iron Curtain, along with the violence that kept it in place for over three quarters of a century, is far from being thrown aside into the rubble of outdated accessories, as some are endeavoring. A *totalitarianism of inconsistency* appears capable of casting doubt on even the memories of this historic time. In this system, not only is everything the equivalent of everything else, but also nothing exists unless it is everything's equivalent, and vice versa.

12

THE REJECTION OF THE NEGATIVE

Because we of this era have the good fortune to live "in real time," there is nothing left to anticipate. Everything foreseen by even the most dismal of prophets is catching up with us. Indeed, it is arriving at the galloping speed of triumphant stupidity, as shown in Pierre Lévy's *World philosophie.* This book has the merit of openly displaying everything about which the most relentless defenders of progress have prudently guarded their silence. This book teaches us that "individuals become businesses,"[1] but also that "businesses become universities,"[2] to the point of confusing "the ideas of business and the business of ideas"[3]—all to the great joy of the author, who is obviously a positive hero of the kind our age is trying to make commonplace.

Reading further in the book, we come upon several discoveries: "To understand cultural and social evolution, we should not look toward the past but toward the future, in the direction evolution is taking."[4] Meanwhile, we should not overlook some truths that are difficult to swallow. "Because it is the inertia of divergence, history—the past that still lives within the present—is almost always opposed to the peace and reunification of humanity."[5] Subsequently, here and there, we find observations, casually strewn, that prompt us to wonder how we could have lived so long without ever reaching such conclusions. For example, the "classic universities find themselves in the same position as small businessmen in the wake of the large chains that offer a greater selection for a better price and pander to their customers by enrolling them in 'clubs' packed with advantages."[6] And this is especially noteworthy: "Social classes exist only in the kingdom of concupiscence."[7]

But let's not let this stop us, swimming like an ahistorical fish in the worst kind of Teilhard de Chardinian soup,* Pierre Lévy is convinced that "the computer is the fire of the future,"[8] and that the multiplicity of forms it engenders will lead us not to the end of history, as certain hucksters suggest, but to "the very form of love," which is (here is something we did not know before) the apotheosis of cyberculture. This, in fact, is the final message of this prophetic book: "As the universe draws away from the time of the material Big Bang, human freedom brings it toward a spiritual Big Bang that will carry it into the dimension of love."[9] Now this is definitely reassuring!

Nevertheless, ridiculous as it appears, this world in which the shadow of the slightest trace of negativity is absent—this world in which "the illusion of individual thought is the preeminent 'idiocy,'" under the highly erudite pretext that "*idiōtēs* in ancient Greek means 'particular,' 'separate,'"[10] this repugnant world of the deranged communication of programmed bliss—is perhaps not so different or far removed from the one in which we live.

This is illustrated by the almost universal silence that accompanied the 1996 French publication of the manifesto *Industrial Society and Its Future,*[11] attributed to the individual the United States had nicknamed the Unabomber, who was regarded for seventeen years as Public Enemy Number One. Its author was the mysterious terrorist who, between 1978 and 1995, sent parcel bombs to the directors of aviation firms as well as to university professors and researchers in the fields of computer science and biology.† Throughout these years, the FBI led an

*[Pierre Teilhard de Chardin (1881–1955) was a French Jesuit priest and paleontologist who dedicated his life trying to integrate the Christian theology and the theories of evolution. —*Ed.*]

†Hence the pseudonym Unabomber given him by the FBI: *Un* for "university" and *a* for "airlines."

active search for him, offering a reward of one million dollars to whoever could supply information leading to his arrest. Their efforts were futile until April 1995, when the Unabomber proposed the following bargain to the *New York Times:* He would cease his terrorist activities if it published, within three months' time, the manifesto he had written against "industrialized society." The FBI vacillated. Almost two months later, the *Washington Post* published the one-hundred-page critique of our world. Six months after this, the Unabomber was exposed (for his own good) by an obscure teacher who was astonished to recognize in this text the tone and ideas of his elder brother, Theodore Kaczynski, a brilliant mathematician who had resigned his position at the University of California, Berkeley, in 1977.

Because the publication through blackmail of this document caused a great commotion in the United States, the hubbub made it all the easier to overlook its content. Furthermore, after it was discussed in anarchist milieus on the Internet and elsewhere, it soon seemed as if this singular theoretician (who was charged with causing three deaths and injuring twenty-three people—all of whom were representatives of the technocratic civilization he said he was fighting) had never written a single line of the text.

On this point, as on so many others, academia set the tone—which seems to confirm the Unabomber's analysis that academics are the best agents of the society they claim to critique. In fact, all the university professors solicited by the police to evaluate the text whose author the law enforcers sought to arrest were unanimous: Not only did this text not fulfill university criteria, but its author was not one of them. For example, the academic Kirkpatrick Sale, "although favorable to anarchist theses" and "hostile to technology," believed this manifesto to be "the work of an embittered individual, who never managed to earn his degree."[12]

These evaluations suggest that the Unabomber should have written this text to please his former colleagues and conform to their derisory criteria! In addition, surely he was not thinking of leftist academics, whom he considered the epitome of false consciousness, when he said he was directing his message to all those who did not want or could not submit to this "oversocialized" world, to all the "rebels without a cause" who were convinced, as he was, that "the revolution against technology will probably have to be a revolution of outsiders, a revolution from below and not from above."[13]

Because this manifesto was not published under the same sensational conditions in France as in the United States, it was all the easier to conceal it. At best, an allusion was made to a "muddled brief against the alienation of industrialized society"[14] in order to avoid accepting that this text, despite its obvious gaffes, constituted a pitiless critique of the technological world to which nearly all people are so well adapted. In fact, this critique was so thorough that not a single journalist picked up on how current events at the time of its publication in France provided a perfect illustration of the author's contentions. This period included the first revelations of mad cow disease, as well as the new discoveries of the true extent of the Chernobyl disaster ten years after it occurred. In addition, countless problems caused by the food industry were just then coming to public notice. The fact remains that while the affair made more noise in the United States (in large part due to the tracking down and arrest of the Unabomber, which aired on every American television channel), the press also avoided making any allusion to the troubling content of the manifesto published several months earlier.

This is no doubt why, in both France and the United States, it is regarded as meaningless that the author took the fatal risk of being unmasked for the sole purpose of seeing his critique published. This is also why his identification by his brother lends credit to the theory of his insanity, which satisfies almost everyone—from the police to the majority of antiestablishment types.

The fact is that the Unabomber was completely in the wrong, primarily for not offering the kind of victim profile that could have been used to excuse even his most serious deviant acts. In fact, this brilliant student who came from an immigrant family of modest means and from parents who had worked hard with the goal of seeing their children attain higher social status, quickly became a mathematician of note at the University of California, Berkeley, only to quit at the age of twenty-six to live a completely solitary life in a Montana cabin. As someone carrying the hopes of this society, it was first and foremost unforgivable for him to disdain the academic glory it offered as well as to avoid claiming any kind of difference that could have justified such a dereliction of duty.

Even more, his fierce defense of nature against industrialized society appeared inadmissible by implying that we must pursue a total rupture with civilization. But what was especially unacceptable was the way in which the fury of this defense refuted the Boy Scout ideology that forms the consensual bedrock of ecological mediocrity. This made him all the more guilty of challenging the good conscience of our age with his criminal violence.

Consequently, he was immediately suspect from the revolutionary standpoint. While it is understandable that the majority of anarchists in the United States, having long renounced violence, would disassociate themselves from his methods if not his ideas, the rejection and even hostility prompted by the publication of his text in France in certain so-called radical milieus has but one explanation: Contrary to the majority of these radicals, the Unabomber accepted the consequences of what he said. No doubt, he had skipped his theory classes. It was even impossible to make any reliable connections between his argument and those texts that are now classic critiques of technology. Being in too great a hurry, he must have decided to write from what he felt, without seeking justification for his sentiments from those authors with serious reputations. He wrote in complete urgency, cobbling together his ideas with the same do-it-yourself approach he used to construct his bombs.

The far-from-trivial consequence of this was the disappearance, as if by magic, of the famous gulf between theory and practice. This embodiment of an implacable consistency in action constituted his imprescriptible crime in a world where, in a half century, the intellectual class had learned to artistically cultivate the separation between what is done and what is said—so much so that this is now established as their personal criterion for excellence.

Thus we can easily understand why people went so far out of their way to try and reduce this entire affair to a trivial news story. In both France and the United States, what stuck was the image of a somewhat deranged scholar, and this prevented people from seeing the fact that the very existence of the Unabomber in itself unmasks the fundamental swindles that the world uses to fabricate its shadow-free positivism. These swindles range from the con game of social progress and the lie of ecological consensus to the scandal of intellectual inconsequentiality. Hence the need to blur the lines about what is truly at stake here, with retouching and even falsification. The unacceptable must be concealed: This society, founded on the rejection of all negativity, nevertheless could produce an individual who denied it absolutely—even the fictional forms of protest it offers.

13

VIRTUAL POSITIVITIES AND NEGATIVITIES

For those of us who are disgruntled and who have grown alarmed at this systematic erasure of all trace of negativity, our era easily meets our objections with an impressive sampling of deviant activities, revolts, rebellions, and perversions of all kinds. It could even be said that it cultivates them. In addition, everything becomes more or less subversive. It is likely that hopes of prompting us to follow this movement, aided by the fine spring weather of the year 2000, led to the installation of a kind of subversive fauna—images of fantasy animals—on the platforms of the Paris Metro, where things really do appear to be taking place between muggings. This is how we have finally reached the age of state-aided subversion.

The 1999 publication of a dictionary entitled *Le Siècle rebelle* [The Rebel Century],[1] offered a catalog of individuals and movements that have known how to swim against the tide. This "dictionary of protest" is primarily a dictionary of confusion. We can find just about anything within its pages—from *Tel Quel* and the New Age to Francis Ponge and Edgar Morin* (though, obviously, better rebels and centers of revolt could have been chosen)—and all entries are placed on the same level as

*[*Tel Quel* was a French avant-garde literary journal founded by Philippe Sollers. Francis Ponge, a French poet and essayist, made contacts with the surrealists and for a decade belonged to the Communist Party. Edgar Morin was a French philosopher and sociologist who maintained connections with the surrealists and the Communists. —*Ed.*]

those rebels who remain impossible to ignore, and who are most often represented here by nobodies.

In any case, truly rebellious individuals are rare exceptions among all the others who have to be really worked up to warrant inclusion in the dictionary. We can note, for instance, that Nobel Prize winners have found a home in this text, whether the "very politically correct" Dario Fo or the Stalinist cop Pablo Neruda. On the other hand, René Crevel does not appear at all. Nor does the poet Benjamin Péret, a French army deserter and convicted felon in three different countries; he is merely mentioned offhandedly here and there for his participation in Dada and surrealism, as well as for writing a "hysterically anticlerical poem."[2] Arthur Cravan, Jacques Vaché, and Jacques Rigaut serve a similar minor role under the title (very contestable under these circumstances) of "Three Suicided by Society." Yet the more than dubious Bertolt Brecht sits enthroned above three whole columns of text, and the equally questionable hussars (Jacques Laurent, Antoine Blondin, Roger Nimier, and Michel Déon) get a full-page display. We may well ask, however, whether it is better to be overlooked entirely than to appear in such an anthology in which Georges Bataille is described as a "French writer" but Antonin Artaud is depicted as a "boundaries writer." Perhaps this provides an inkling of the new idea of a borderless culture.

As for the exactitude presiding over the creation of this work, it reaches new heights with the entries "Interactivity" and "Avant-Gardes." As for "Avant-Gardes," however, the author did his homework, considering that his thoughts are framed by two flashes of lightning. On one side is Jacques Derrida: "The effect of the avant-garde is always decipherable after the fact. Thus the avant-garde, if there is one, is impossible to present." On the other side is Philippe Sollers: "An avant-garde is in some way a kind of rationality in advance . . . an ideological and poetic barometer." Confronted by these observations, we can be only grateful to Alfred Jarry, who, fatigued in advance by all the ineptitude fostered by the notion of avant-garde, convinced us of the beauties to be found in the "literature of the hindquarters."

To return to this depressing dictionary: Its alphabetical classification is of no help at all, and it is no surprise to find all the deleterious effects of the *order of promiscuity* displayed in close order. This allows us to see the extent to which the sinister effects of this promiscuity affect time. They impose laughable lines of descent: Ubu is declared forefather of Oulipo,* while Alexandre Jacob's "libertarian individualism"† is "later recycled by the situationists and the Enragés of '68."§[3]

The idea of recycling alone provides us the last word on the text: *Le Siècle rebelle* aims to "recycle" everything that has not yet been recuperated. The back cover only confirms this: "In seeking to understand our era through its rebels, we have endeavored to remain resolutely optimistic." Here is a book that transforms the negative into the positive. More precisely, it invents a new data bank by making virtual negativities of the ideas, gestures, attitudes, and feelings that elsewhere are ranked as outdated accessories.

Perhaps these negativities are inseparable from the production of the virtual positivities mentioned here earlier with regard to metaphor. Essentially, these two kinds of linguistic references exist as decoys. This point plays such a determinative role in defining what has taken the place of the ethical landscape that it is one I will revisit.

From these decoys, and from a different angle, we can consider this matter as one aspect of the sad chronicle of vanishing species. As soon as zoologists informed us that "for several decades . . . the great blue whale

*[Ubu is the main character in three Alfred Jarry plays (*King Ubu, Ubu Cuckolded,* and *Ubu Enchained*) that satirize European philosophies. Oulipo (standing for Ouvroir de literature potentielle), founded in 1960, was a group of French writers who created works using constrained writing techniques in order to trigger inspiration and ideas. —*Ed.*]

†[Alexandre Jacob (1879–1954), also known as Marius Jacob, was a French anarchist and burglar. —*Ed.*]

§Situationism held that individuals are influenced more by external—situational—factors than by internal motives. The Enragés of '68 emerged in France in 1968 at Nanterre University. Strongly influenced by the situationists, they played a leading role in the French insurrection of May 1968. —*Ed.*]

population has not been recovering in the Antarctic Ocean, although the species has been strictly protected there since the beginning of the 1960s,"[4] it became analogically clear that the new encyclopedic interest in rebels has not at all contributed to their reappearance.

More important, while today zoologists note that the numbers of great blue whales has "decreased by a factor of 100," whereas "that of penguins and Weddell seals have grown [in the same waters] in a significant and sometimes substantial way during the last half century,"[5] we find that the case of the rebels has proceeded no differently: They seem to have been replaced by the very people studying them. Like the prospering of penguins and seals at the expense of the great cetaceans, there are now countless professors, art historians, and well-established writers who have made a specialty out of exploiting the negative in order to win their doctorates in radicalism. This is somewhat parallel to the disappearance of the great blue whale. Just as "various species have [in reality] occupied the food niche freed by the decline in numbers of this whale, primarily consuming the plankton that make up krill," which represents "the sole food of the great rorquals,"[6] through their consumption of the plankton of words and forms that was once the food of the rebels, a new species of intellectuals and artists now occupies a cultural niche to which its creators—the rebels themselves—can never return.

All of this refers to an important factor in the mechanics of the extinction of animal species—and perhaps even more, of the disappearance of some intellectual species—and could explain today's absence of revolt. Just as "the introduction of cats and/or rats into certain Pacific Islands inhabited by seabirds that nest on the ground or in burrows has been fatal to certain petrel species and other oceanic avian species,"[7] once new "inhabitants" were introduced into the cultural niche of the negative, they gradually managed to impose their own living conditions there. The surrounding environment was modified according to the needs of these new arrivals, and these new living conditions were fatal to the original inhabitants.

■

The result has not been a ferocious struggle for the life of thought, as we would have seen in a different era, but instead the appearance of a new, greedy, needy intellectual fauna. This new "species" was ever ready to instigate those "social debates" (one of the major fictions of our time). In these debates, pseudocriticism practices at leisure in order to mislead the small fry and thereby conceal the motive—influenced by the reality overload—provided by and propagated by those framing these debates.

We can observe this in any controversy over art in which, in order to avoid questioning the appalling insignificance of modernity, some support the celebration of the art of deep roots and tradition while others defend an in-name-only avant-garde.

It is telling, however, that both sides have refrained from pronouncing their views on the international success of Yasmina Reza's play *Art.** This piece is a clever extract of hysterical mediocrity, shrewd small-mindedness, and self-satisfied stupidity that has given new life to an old hatred against the desire for freedom that has haunted modern art. This hatred is never absent from the party of reason and the back rooms of the shops of the happy medium.

What is the secret of this *lateral critique,* the origin of all the illusionary confrontations put on for our amusement? We must never contrast sharply with our alleged object. In fact, whatever the stakes might be, the sole reason for the existence of this lateral critique is to prevent anyone from getting to the bottom of whatever problem has been broached. Just as any recourse to a virtual positivity invokes values that no longer have any currency—as we have seen concerning metaphor—so also these are *trompe l'oeil* debates that allow for the production of a virtual negativity.

We might laugh at all of this, especially when we note that on just about any subject—information in real time, in vitro insemination, computer crime—the gravity of the pundits speaking, like that of wres-

*[Yasmina Reza, born May 1, 1959, is a French author and actress whose play *Art* debuted in 1995. It has been performed worldwide and received numerous awards. —*Trans.*]

tlers in wrestling's heyday, is directly proportional to the rigged nature of the confrontation. It is not visible to many of us, however, that antagonistic viewpoints are often presented for the sole purpose of establishing their reciprocal neutralization. From here, we are but one step away from setting up a dialogue between torturers and victims. Such a step was already taken at the beginning of 1999, when Abu Abbas Abdi, instigator of the hostage-taking at the American embassy in Tehran twenty years earlier, met one of his former victims on television so that he might "dialogue" with her.

The consequence: The very notion of objectivity is altered if not adulterated, as shown by the fact that every one of these confrontations has ended by establishing that objectivity now consists of splitting right and wrong equally between each opponent.

Thus, *for* and *against* have become an inseparable couple, like Laurel and Hardy or Pat and Patachon—perhaps the most legitimate couple of all, in an age that generates virtual positivities and negativities on demand, like so many interfaces of an increasingly redundant reality. We are led to believe that the reality overload cannot truly prosper without these virtual values. And these values preside over all the evasions that accompany a new way of thinking: *the rationality of inconsistency.*

14

THE RATIONALITY OF INCONSISTENCY

While various authorities of the United Nations eventually adopted the International Accord on Biological Diversity at the Rio conference of 1992, which assigned to its member governments the obligation of preserving the biodiversity of all the territory under their authority, the years that followed have revealed what little actual effect this agreement has actually had. But the years have also revealed how the unrestrained logging of forests, the intensive cultivation of fragile soils, and the extermination of plant and animal populations every day are repeated in the extermination of ideas. Indeed, even poetry, long perceived as a symbol of an intact life, imperceptibly accustoms us to devastation so that we are more completely deceived as to the actual state of our surroundings.

This deception has apparently succeeded; today, no one seems to notice how any given intellectual, political, or moral choice is counterbalanced by its opposite. Indeed, it seems natural for morality to answer to permissiveness, fundamentalism to multiculturalism, devotion to cynicism, sectarianism to centrism, fetishism to indifference, the quest for the *hard* to the *cool* sensation, the concern for security to the taste for risk. What is surprising is that these antagonisms have managed to coexist not only within a group, but also within a single individual, at the mercy of this rationality of inconsistency. We adopt this new way of thinking without recognizing it as the very rationale of our "connectionist" world.

Yet despite the scant attention this phenomenon has drawn, there is good reason to fear the ease with which so many people seem increasingly to conform to behavioral models forged only a few years ago in corporate headquarters. In 1992, it was written that "the image of the chameleon may describe the pro who knows how to handle his interpersonal relations in such a way that he can easily identify with other people's viewpoints," and that "this kind of adaptability is surely the key to penetrating the network mind."[1] Remarkably, even the most serious-minded observers today have accepted as a major assumption in our societies that "it is . . . realistic, in a networked world, to be ambivalent . . . because the situations we must face are themselves complex and uncertain."[2] But they do not neglect to point out that this merely amounts to the "sacrifice . . . of the personality as a way of being that displays similar attitudes and behavior in any and all circumstances."[3]

This changes everything—so much so that standing up in protest (something I haven't given up yet) becomes obsolete when we are faced with the backpedaling of a certain intellectual who, after having been a Maoist, is now a champion of social democracy while still proclaiming his radical nature. Or when we must deal with someone who, after having been an adherent to dialectical materialism, now finds his bliss in Christian thought while striving to reconcile the two. As for deploring the rise of a considerable number of former leftists to positions of authority, we should recognize this as the reflection of an aspiration "to feel in step," which, lamentable as it may be, has become the hallmark of an entire generation. This group of people from a certain age is incapable of seeing how discouraging such reversals can be; in such a short time, they have become accustomed to the coexistence of apparently incompatible elements.

We cannot say too often, however, how well the inconsequentiality of those who claim to be the intellectuals and artists of our time has prepared the terrain. We must also recall the school of servile versatility that a good portion of the intelligentsia attended happily over the last half century through their adherence to Marxism-Leninism—or at least, through their failure to set themselves clearly apart from it. This creates a precedent.

Accordingly, it is significant that people today are bored by any recollection of the unforgivable straying of many such individuals. Today, there exists a tendency not to overlook the ignominious behavior of an Aragon* or the indefensible positions of a Sartre. Figures like these are revisited with the intention of finding another meaning for their choices, independent of the actual consequences of these choices. We can see this tendency in Sartre's current "revival": Never before has so much emphasis been placed on the insignificant nature of the most serious contradictions found in one mind.

Artistic irresponsibility has always received good press and been an excuse for the worst kind of behavior. In addition, philosophical irresponsibility is regarded as both a precondition for a school of thought and a sign of its wealth. Accordingly, it is interpreted that the greater Sartre's errors, the more intense his quest for freedom. How many other somewhat tarnished intellectual coats of arms will soon find themselves gilded again in this way—and at such little expense? In a four-part television interview described as "fascinating," the philosopher Jean-Toussaint Desanti, whose Stalinist ties are no secret to anyone, informs us, "[P]hilosophy is a remedy against being duped all the time."[4] Let the word be spread!

As for the avant-garde, perhaps it is incapable of rediscovering its most controversial meaning. The most tortuous trajectories of today's prominent thinkers and artists appear to foreshadow the new lifestyle to which we are increasingly invited to conform.

Because of these illustrious examples, we now know that "in order to adjust to a 'connectionist' world, we must display sufficient flexibility."[5] It is not hard to convince us that "permanency, especially regard-

*[Louis Aragon (1887–1982) was a member of the French surrealist group until the early thirties, at which point he broke with the group to toe the official line of the French Communist Party—for which he played a major cultural role until the end of his life. —*Trans.*]

ing ourselves or any lasting attachment to 'values,' is open to criticism as an incongruous, even pathological, rigidity and, depending on the context, as inefficient, rude, and intolerant, and evidence of an inability to communicate."[6] We think we are hearing Philippe Sollers presenting his theory of libertinism, which supposedly justifies the way he turns his coat, his sleeves, and his pockets inside out. This is given such emphasis that, though this plasticity is not the sole quality required of the "connectionist" man, who, passing from one network to another, should be able to continue to be "someone," the price of entry to this new form of excellence is the abandonment of all critical attitudes.

This is clearly explained by Pierre Lévy in his manual for the perfect connectionist:

> The critical attitude looks to the past. It manufactures an increasingly schizophrenic and unhappy consciousness in that each of us actively takes part in the condemned movement in our own way. Furthermore, the legitimacy of this critique has been largely usurped. It rests on a deceptive incorporation into the great philosophical critique of the seventeenth, eighteenth, and nineteenth centuries, which magnanimously looked to the future, in opposition to conservatism, and denounced the forces holding back humanity's march to emancipation. On the other hand, the major part of the contemporary "critique" of capitalist globalization, cyberculture, and the technosciences unfortunately works harder at spreading resentment and hate than at promoting a positive vision for the future.[7]

This quote may be a little long, but how could I pass over this opportunity to learn what we ought not to do?

It has become even easier to believe that all—from the slightest whim to the heaviest theoretical formulation—can coexist, just as books on windsurfing, Cistercian abbeys, Rollerblading, and the Quattrocento coexist on the shelves of large chain bookstores. In addition, there is little point in continuing to deplore the loss of a hierarchy of values. The lateral critique, however, continues in this vein, clinging to its anachronistic criteria in order to continue stabbing the waves with its sword. Yet we should be equally disturbed by the sensorial mutilation that goes hand in hand with the affirmation of the rationality of inconsistency, which relies on the order of promiscuity that it reinforces through its exaltation of the diverse.

Just as placing poetry within the reach of everyone basically means isolating the poem from all—both within and outside of ourselves—that can feed it, there is no longer any idea, feeling, or belief that, to be accepted, can be exempt from receiving similar treatment. In other words, an idea must now be redrawn along a dotted line that makes it an option equivalent to any other. At the same time, the effect of this is to enclose in an illusion all those who choose this option—because even the choice is presented as so essential that there is no reason to concern ourselves with its concrete and sensorial implications.

This has been taken so far that there is no longer any fundamental difference between the thoughtlessness of the new fashion for off-trail skiing—resulting in the avalanches that have recently buried winter resorts—and the thoughtlessness of Élisabeth Badinter* when she denounces the dangers of parity after writing, in 1986, in *L'Un est l'autre* [The One Is the Other]: "Our mutant hearts no longer seek the pangs of desire. It could almost be said we have no other choice. The model of resemblance works hand in hand with the eradication of desire."[8] In both cases, the same irresponsibility characterizes the choice of ideas or behaviors that is constructed similarly, despite any consideration outside their immediate affirmation. Avalanches are not nearly as catastrophic as the varied effects of this instigation of the "eradication of desire."

By now, we can guess that this rationality of inconsistency is also a rationality of thoughtlessness, the source of many of the "dysfunc-

*[Élisabeth Badinter is a French writer, feminist, and philosophy professor at the École Polytechnique in Paris. —*Trans.*]

tions," to use the accepted term, that now make up current events but are actually equivalent to chains of political disasters (the war in the former Yugoslavia), economic disasters (mad cow disease), and intellectual disasters (a minister of culture refers to a program he has developed for "inspiring a desire for culture").[9] Many continue to take pains to avoid any parallels between these "dysfunctions" and any kind of natural disaster. All the better to conceal the thoughtlessness that is the price we pay for the civilization of the diverse being foisted upon us.

This may prompt us to wonder about the role played by ecological discourse in biodiversity. Here, Charles Fourier's reservations come to mind: "I believe no more in the virtues of the shepherds than I do in those of their apologists." The question then becomes whether or not this insistence on biodiversity may give the semblance of a natural basis for the glorification of eclecticism in which convictions, enthusiasms, and passions are nothing more than a question of tastes and colors.

In addition, under pretense of connecting all, the "connectionist" world breaks, erases, or distorts the logical, sensorial, and organic bonds among individuals and things. This seems to be the new law of the jungle imposed by the reality overload: Promiscuity has gained the upper hand over interdependence. It could well be that the ecological discourse on biodiversity thus plays the role of a virtual positivity that serves to mask a dictatorship of the diverse. This dictatorship relies on the rationality of inconsistency's ability to offer everybody the unprecedented possibility of manufacturing an absolute out of anything and everything.

15

RELATIVE ABSOLUTES

Arthur Cravan said: "I've dreamed of being great enough to found and fashion a republic all to myself." All those claiming to affirm their difference—by gathering together in search of resemblance—would be hard put to proclaim this as Arthur Cravan had.

A growing number of similar groups—neofeminists, gays, Creolitarians—have deliberately chosen the cultural realm in which to find reasons for establishing a system of exclusion that also aims at assimilation. This seeming contradiction is not a contradiction at all: It is the distinguishing mark of relative absolutes, thanks to which today there is no longer any difference that cannot be presented as the key to the world.

It would remain just another oddity if the affirmation of an identity did not represent the sole political alternative to the "connectionist world"—at least, according to those who are most clued in to the "network society."* At the beginning of a work entitled *Le Pouvoir de l'identité* [The Power of Identity], Manuel Castells writes: "Two opposing forces are battling to remodel our world and our lives: globalization and identity."[1] Given that identity is redefined as "the process of constructing meaning

*Among whom I number Manuel Castells, Alain Touraine, Luc Boltanski, and Ève Chiapello.

from one cultural attribute, or a coherent grouping of attributes, which takes priority over all other sources"[2]—in other words, the structuring force that creates meaning—it is surprising that not one of these sociologists has pointed out the amazing reinterpretation of Western thought and art generated in the last decade by the notion of finding our identity. This is undoubtedly most predominant in the Anglo-Saxon world, with women's studies, Native American studies, gay and lesbian studies, and so forth, which determine university instruction as well as how bookstores and libraries categorize their books. Still, even though the rest of the world has been late to catch on, it has not missed out. Here and there, "targeted" literature is put forth, and books are already being written for Breton butchers, Danube peasants, and one-legged mountain climbers.

In the meantime, a new form of cretinization has appeared on the scene. It even held its assizes at the Louvre from April to July 2000, with the exhibition *Possessing and Destroying: Sexual Strategies in Western Art.* Here we learn straight off, before seeing a single image, that

> Western art can speak of sex in only one way: violently. Rape might be an even better way of putting it. The sexual obsession of Western art is *rape* . . . woman consistently and literally plays the role of a whipping boy. . . . It is a *repressive* art. What it reveals is not sex so much as power. It is a *psychopathic* art. It can experience pleasure only through constraint. [It represents] painful voluptuousness, tragic pleasure."*

Once we discover that this exhibition's commissioner is a male and not a female curator, it may be easier to understand why I prefer to return to primary sources.

■

*These words, appearing on the didactic posters advertising this exhibition, were reprinted in the press file.

About ten years ago, I was privileged to witness the manufacture of one of these relative absolutes that now hold sway in all realms.

Under the pretext that "analysis of woman's place in culture demands a radical deconstruction of art history and the production of a new discourse that surpasses sexism, as opposed simply to replacing it with its opposite,"[3] I heard Griselda Pollock, an art historian, argue on behalf of "the frontality of the subject." To her mind, this frontality was a characteristic of the paintings by women as varied as Berthe Morisot, Maria Cazals, and Madame Vigée-Lebrun in that historically, these artists had been deprived of their own space and were constrained to paint on the fly. They used kitchen tables or pantries—from which Pollock deduces a "sense of spatial intimacy" that is totally absent from paintings by men. Thus this intimacy is obviously absent from Picasso's famous painting that was rebaptized for the occasion as *The Hideous Women of Avignon*.

As we may guess, Picasso was not the sole victim of this deconstruction—and Degas, Toulouse-Lautrec, and Manet were disqualified immediately for having supplied degrading images of women, whether their subject was an object of desire, contemplation, or cold observation. The conference attendees preferred the inevitable maternity scenes that burden the paintings of that period with their lack of imagination and their inanity and bore us with their tedious repetition of the same "edifying" images. It is not as if these women artists did not participate in the system of values this conference was claiming to deconstruct. Actually, in their work they exalted representations of women who were in no way as free as those inspired by the desire, boredom, or even distrust of artists such as Degas and Manet. These disqualified artists revealed the grace of an arm that moves forward like the break of day, the sudden unveiling of a perspective through the play of a curved hip, the stupor that comes from a certain manner of sitting, and the dizzying sparkle of "eyes polished by brandy," as Baudelaire says.

This is precisely what the leaders of the conference were striving to ignore in order to deny what Degas, Toulouse-Lautrec, and Manet observed and then had succeeded in wresting from the psychosocial representation and conventional role of woman. But there is no point here in deploring the distressing blindness of these specialists in deconstruction. Their work consists of the complete occultation of whatever subversive force continues to be at work in the magisterial evocations of desire found in Manet's *Olympia* and Picasso's *Demoiselles d'Avignon.*

In fact, this occultation seems to be the real goal of these "reinterpretations" in which the difference is emphasized only so far as it lends greater credence to the existing order. A maternity scene will always be more reassuring than the *Demoiselles d'Avignon.* Likewise, we can prefer not to envision the way representation in Picasso's painting staggers under the savagery of the desire that seems to take modernity hostage in the work. Surely it is much simpler to praise, along with Marilyn French, the fact that her neofeminist peers "point out the woman hatred in the work of painters such as Willem de Kooning and Picasso. Whether they paint women with this hatred or idealize them or vapidly sentimentalize them (as Renoir does) or lend them cold superiority (as Degas does), they are implicitly assaulting female reality and autonomy."[4]

The tendency to allow ourselves to be seduced by this kind of deconstruction allows us to evaluate the progress of this rationality of inconsistency. Likewise, the deconstruction can develop in a culture whose essential role is to produce interpretations of the world that serve to prevent anyone from understanding it, and even more so from changing it.

I received an unexpected illustration of this by the obviously foolhardy commissioner of the exhibition *Possessing and Destroying: Sexual Strategies in Western Art.* Before condemning Michelangelo, Signorelli, and Rembrandt for shameless sexism, and then adding Ingres, Degas, and Picasso, he informed us that for our own good "[t]he apparatus of the state thinks for you. Revolt against it. Look for yourself. . . . And if this discourse offends you, contest it. Or don't think about it." This was a charming admonition, modern and capable of being taken at face value or anywhere up to second, third, or thirty-sixth degree; but it is doomed to remain null and void for the obvious moral reason that, as the surrealists wrote in their *Open Letter to Paul Claudel* in 1925, "no one can be both an ambassador of France and a poet," or, even less, be both "head curator of the graphic arts department" at the Louvre Museum *and* a rebel. In other words, we cannot be part of the system *and* against it. But the rationality of inconsistency makes no such distinction.

Here it is permissible to ask if it is totally fortuitous that the affirmation of identity has begun to assume this form, at a time when, promoted by museums worldwide, "installation fitters" promise innovation by exhibiting the indigence of worlds dramatically closed upon themselves but still proliferating rapidly enough to occupy the entire field of the possible. It is definitely not far from the squared spaces of Jean-Pierre Raynaud to neofeminist doxa, but I cannot help but note how their followers would have contributed, from one installation to the next, to establishing as self-evident a mode of affirmation that plays on the exclusion of everything else.

Jus as this kind of artistic approach, which always claims to be rebellious, adapts quite well to the norms of the museum—to the extent that its existence outside this institutional space is inconceivable—every group identity today plays on its difference . . . and all the better to conform to the status quo. Just as installation artists, satisfied with the conditional freedom of occasionally marking the spaces at their disposal with a few disappointing objects, have no intention of instigating any sort of rupture, the identity partisans of every stripe seem to have no thought of changing the game, rushed as they are merely to rearrange a few pieces on the board for their own benefit. We can conclude, then, that this quest for identity in difference simply strengthens the existing order.

This fact does not escape Léo Bersani, who, in *Homos,* is compelled by the depth of his reflections to set against the opinion of Michel Foucault his notion of the existence of "a continuity between the political structures of oppression and the erotic economy of the body."[5] Michel Foucault considers "the strategic relationships of power in S/M as a convention of pleasure."[6] This makes it difficult for him to accept the new "stubborn persistence" of gays and lesbians "to convince society that they can be good parents, good soldiers, and good priests."[7] This, however, is an ultraminority viewpoint that collides with almost everything existing today as identity-based philosophy—even if, as can be seen in France with the recent PACS* debates, the homophobic morality of those adversaries to civil unions has somewhat occulted the new conformity in which homosexual identity seeks to drape itself. Accordingly, we have witnessed a curious sight in which both sides compete in an effort to make the most anachronistically dogged defense of the family, a concept that certain idealists have been trying to annihilate for more than a century.

Yet after having been forced week after week to swallow this indigestible pap of high sentiment sprinkled with symbolism, this gay and nongay defense of the family, the situation is somewhat alleviated when several gays† state that they see in the homosexual claim to the right to marry the betrayal of the principles that were fundamental to the founding of the gay movement during the 1970s. I admit to feeling a certain thrill when recalling Guy Hocquenghem's *L'Après-mai des faunes,*§ which suggests "gliding from one order to another by following their flaws." I know—times have changed. This was even followed by the anti-identity endeavor of the queer, supported by the speculation of Judith Butler. For Butler, cross-dressing was the liberating interrogation of sexual identity and acquired a political value to the extent that "the

*[*Pacte civil de solidarité*, a contract of civil union under French law for same-sex or opposite-sex couples. —*Ed.*]

†In particular, Michael Warner in *Gay and Lesbian Quarterly* 5, no. 2 (1999). I have no problem saying that in 1996 I signed—and would sign again today—the *Manifesto for the Recognition of the Homosexual Couple.* In my eyes, marriage is a convenience that, like any other, should be taken advantage of if the need arises. As far as believing in it, that's something else entirely.

§[The title means *The After-May of the Fauns. After-May* refers to the time following the May 1968 uprisings in France. The title is also a play on the poem "L'après-midi d'un faune" by Stéphane Mallarmé, and *faune* in French, besides referring to the mythical creature, can also be a pejorative term for a mob, crowd, or group. —*Ed.*]

normative focus for a gay and lesbian practice ought to be on the subversive and parodic redeployment of power, rather than on the impossible fantasy of its full-scale transcendence."[8] But this was in 1990. Since then, Judith Butler has reached the point of "asking if the parody of dominant norms is enough to displace them, and if the denaturalization of sexual identity may have the effect of consolidating hegemonic norms."[9]

The fact remains that the organization Queer Nation still seeks to blur the borders of sexual roles themselves without disrupting their normalizing mechanism. Michael Warner notes that "the idea of community remains problematic . . . because a large part of gay and lesbian history is one of an absence of community, and because dispersion rather than localization continues to be the determining factor in queer self awareness."[10] Finally, Léo Bersani refuses "to return to immobilizing definitions of identity" and places the emphasis on "a certain inaptitude of gay desire for sociality such as it is."[11] This is surely the most important contribution of his study, and it appears significant that in the final analysis, despite all the efforts to escape the identity cage, the current state of gay realization has not succeeded at all. To the contrary, it falls back into the catastrophic ideological options of neofeminism—morality included—that I denounced twenty years ago[12] when I emphasized how the boys of the Front homosexual d'action revolutionnaire (FHAR)* distinguished themselves from neofeminism.

Thus it is all the more sad to note that Didier Éribon strives to muddy the waters in his *Réflexions sur la question gay* [*Insult and the Making of the Gay Self*] by advancing the notion that "'subversion' is to be henceforth conceded to gays and lesbians, on condition that they do not leave this identity cage. This tends to underscore the fact that what

*[The FHAR was a short-lived movement in 1971 Paris. It was begun as a lesbian/feminist group, which formed a coalition with male homosexuals. It gave radical visibility to homosexuals, and it sought the overturning of chauvinistic and homophobic values. As the power of men in the group grew, many women left to form splinter groups. —*Ed.*]

is truly subversive today is the refusal of our designated and expected social role."[13] It is as if the violence directed toward homosexuals is not inherent within the fundamental values of this world—the world into which Didier Éribon so desperately wishes to see gays integrated. This means there will likely be little difficulty in swelling the ranks of the choir of "Free Men" who inhabit the already overflowing kingdom of *Ubu enchaîné:**

> We are free. Let's not forget, it's our duty to be free. Hey! Not so fast, or we might arrive on time. Freedom means never arriving on time—never never!—for our freedom drills. Let's disobey together. No! Not together. The first will disobey on the count of one, the second on two, the third on three. That makes all the difference.[14]

What we have here is *integrated difference.*

Along the way, we can note how identity replaces individuality so that such an affirmation favors the implementation of the reality overload. This is favored if only by abolishing all distance between individuals henceforth called upon to line up in equivalent groups whose differences fit together like so many puzzle pieces—but it is a puzzle that does not allow room for anything else.

In the same way, we can assume, after seeing the art of the past ten years adorning its galloping eclecticism sitting with few subversive attributes within the institutional enclosure. The multiplicity of differences exhibited therein, to the point of caricature, exist only to prompt a symbolic consensus by means of the simulacrum of the reality overload. "The more the game accepts the rules, the less it urges their transgression,"[15] Catherine Millet notes as a characteristic of the relative freedom granted to artists within the closed world of the museographical society.

There is no choice but to accept that between the claim of artistic

*[This refers to Alfred Jarry's play *Ubu Enchained.* See footnote, chapter 13, page 84. —*Ed.*]

difference and the claim of identity difference . . . there is no difference. Furthermore, nothing prevents the recognition within both claims that the strength of the grip of a rationality of inconsistency has managed to win mass acceptance of the cause-and-effect relationship between difference and integration—with all the profound depoliticalization it implies.

16

SUBTRACTIVE AESTHETIC

In *Ubu enchaîné* [Ubu Enchained], Alfred Jarry writes: "Madam, my female, I know exactly what I am doing, and you—you don't know what you are talking about." Once again, the competence of this expert on the subject of voluntary servitude provides a hint of what is pushed to the side by the majority of rationalist critics who denounce the aberration of identity "rereadings." These critics, however, do not emphasize the gap between freedom proclaimed and the way in which it is expressed. This is an unfortunate characteristic of everything that claims its difference today. And because this difference can cover everything from rollermania to age brackets to philately, providing a perpetually discounted substitute for identities, it is somewhat alarming that nobody seems overly concerned about it.

Fifty years ago no one was in a position to grasp what kind of poison was at work beneath the pretentious style of socialist realism, or how the partisans of "proletarian art" were drawing from the same sources as the Nazis. Their grievances against "bourgeois art," to complicate matters further, were confused with what the fascists had denounced as "degenerate art." So today no one seems capable of assessing the nature of the reactions—in every sense of the word—that are being provoked in the domain of sensibility under the pretext of restoring to oppressed groups their belittled identities.

■

It would be difficult to find another explanation for the hate that fuels the recent attacks on the poetry of Aimé Césaire perpetrated by the West Indians who uphold the Creole identity. These people have attacked Césaire on the basis that his *Notebook of a Return to My Native Land* could "be the protest statement of any suffering people." Their appalling reasoning: "[I]f the Quebecois were able to adopt it in the 60s, it is because it was not deeply stamped by the West Indies. Furthermore, it was translated into Arabic, and enjoyed great success among the Palestinians."[1] What must be perfectly clear is that this text, which Césaire intended as "a flag of rage and despair," has the major defect of developing into an ungovernable "voyage to the ends of the self that leads us to discover the beyond and the everywhere."[2]

In reality, its poetic power is what has earned such reproaches of the work, obviously because this power makes it impossible to reduce the text to the kind of identity standards recognized and promoted by all sides today. But also, the waterproof quality necessary for the relative absolutes, produced by these identity standards, strictly excludes anything from their domain that might smack of the indeterminate, potential, or passionately distraught through which we can escape ourselves and discover the other within. What could be more natural than to require from words and forms all that we expect of individuals? However, this has the serious consequence of revealing that all of these identity-based readings flush out their enemy in the very element that has provided the history of representation with some of its most splendid peaks of freedom.

It is all the more interesting that people could hardly believe their ears when Cindy Sherman—an artist esteemed by the neofeminists—attacked those "old surrealist things" and their "pretty images."[3] It is obvious that she was thinking of Hans Bellmer, whose work she plagiarizes constantly in order to disguise the pusillanimity of a feminist protest that her photomontages reduce to the repetitious reversal of masculine and feminine elements. In her work, instead of noting what was once called "the survival of the sign in the thing signified," we find ourselves in the presence of a falsifying misappropriation of Bellmer's project. One project is his *Doll,* the "articulated minor" that he invented in 1933. Another work, *Games,* opened previously unknown perspectives of the first "anatomy of the physical unconscious," leading us to realize that "the imagination draws exclusively from physical experience," as well as to the discovery that "desire takes its point of departure, when concerning the intensity of its images, not from a perceptive whole but from one detail."[4]

This is precisely what Cindy Sherman strives to ignore. She is incapable of escaping the hackneyed reuse of an ideological opposition of the masculine and the feminine. She can only twist their symbols for political ends in such a way as to fight not male domination, but the strength of a desire that was a prodigious inventor of forms—the kind of forms that Bellmer showed us in his work by revealing that "the body is comparable to a sentence that invites you to disarticulate it, for the purpose of recombining its actual contents through a series of endless anagrams."[5]

Only when we realize that Bellmer made the decision to build his doll in Nazi Germany, and from that point on he performed no socially useful activity, can we truly assess the value of the insubordination of his twofold resolution. Furthermore, the manufacture of this "artificial girl" acquired a long political reach, which was connected to this young mechanical draftsman's irreversible determination to place himself beyond historical redemption. The scope of his desertion is such that there is no way his work can be decently compared to the activity of an artist who says she is fighting against international male supremacy, but who nonetheless has been supported from the beginning of her career by a considerable number of museum institutions.

This is a good illustration of the now customary way in which deconstructionism is claimed less as a motive for undoing [*defaire*] than for counterfeiting [*contrefaire*]. It is remarkable that copying is now considered an art. Everything, in fact, leads us to believe that the dictatorship of the diverse is modeled on identity-based debraining to impose its dispersed order and recompose our sensory world in accordance with the tastes of a censorship that takes the place of an aesthetic.

This censorship is why this situation is not at all comparable to what emerged with preceding forms of totalitarianism. None of these groups benefits from the support of a state that allows a group to substitute its vision of the world for all other forms of representation. In addition, today we do not find ourselves before the monstrous kitsch of the Soviet or Nazi chromos that imprisoned individuals and things within the light of totalitarian happiness. Consider that the diversified happiness offered us from all sides and in every realm—we are offered opportunities *ad infinitum* to be culturally, culinarily, physically, touristically, and erotically happy—exercises an optimism-based terror from which it is difficult to escape. It is futile to seek a contemporary equivalent to the way in which socialist realism or Nazi art denied the singularity of the individual in order to make it support its ideology.

The novelty now is that while reproduction is no less orchestrated, paradoxically, it appears identical to a *subtractive aesthetic.* Through exposure to advertising, we have long been familiar with this aesthetic, but its theoretical basis lies in the deconstructivist philosophy that purports that nothing has any intrinsic meaning of its own; significance is acquired only from the historical, social, and cultural environment. According to this philosophy, there are no affirmations of identity today that do not result from a dual process of "decontextualization/recontextualization," which rapidly has become part and parcel of the postmodern aesthetic and its borrowing games. The effects of these games are displacement, disorientation, and anachronism.

Under these circumstances, it is no longer surprising to see identity-based groups who conform so easily to the style of domination they pride themselves on fighting. This subtractive aesthetic establishes the conniving nature of these groups' representational systems, which rest on the accumulation of particularities within an original form of censorship. This censorship is quickly replacing all other forms: *imperceptible censorship.*

As much a school of thought as a censorship, the only goal of imperceptible censorship is to replace all consistency with a cut-and-paste technique. Inherent within the triumph of the rationality of inconsistency, it offers the advantage of being the censorship no one sees, for it is applied not to content but to the ability to organize that content in a meaningful manner. As an example, the recent success of the Creolitarian novel, cleverly jury-rigged by the enemies of Aimé Césaire from a patchwork of Creolisms and neoexotica, might correspond to one of those synthesized products whose successive promotions now give rhythm to cultural style. What's more, these relative absolutes are presented as so many elements of a harmonious pluralism. Under the mask of diversity, their conflicting images encourage the diffusion and spread of an operation that repeats itself identically. It is during this operation that deconstruction happily substitutes itself for negation.

We should also note that the multiplicity of these images, otherwise easier to manipulate than the earlier totalitarian chromos, allows what could have been the ferment of revolt to be transformed. As Alfred Jarry proclaims, "We will have public debrainings every Sunday on a hill in the suburbs, with an audience of wooden horses and coconut peddlers." We are done with the old-fashioned desire to reinvent the world. The rationality of inconsistency has found something better. To earn the right to be cited, difference must become the norm—that is, the norm of everything that can be integrated into the mosaic of tastes and colors.

Hence we see the strong modeling provided by these relative absolutes. Furthermore, they allow the development of the swindle of a cultural equality based on the ambiguity between equivalent cultural choices and equality before culture. In addition, this modeling helps reinforce the confusion between horizontality and democracy—a confusion that is upheld cunningly by the image of the network and the fluid nature of what it allegedly transports. Yet there is no use bemoaning the ambiguous nature of this notion of cultural equality, without seeing how it serves as both lid and bulwark to a form of domination whose essential concern is to incorporate everything that is still capable of escaping it.

Because nothing has the right to appear inaccessible anymore, this cultural equality has become a trap for the unwary, and inside this trap any gap must disappear. While increasingly referred to less for giving everyone the ability to gain access to art or poetry than for rendering everyone incapable of perceiving how both may exist only as the power of refusal, the persistent efforts to restore the power of poetry to daily life leave no doubt in this regard. We have even reached the point where a Parisian restaurant, La Coupole, is sponsoring "surrealist" dinners with poetry readings. That we have arrived not at democracy but at the substitution of the *poetry of ambience* for all other forms speaks volumes about the fiction of a cultural equality whose purpose as an indispensable virtual positivity is to destroy both meaning and the negative.

Like a reversal of Rimbaud's decree—"Poetry will no longer give rhythm to action but will precede it"—this intensive promotion of poetry has reached an extreme that cannot be separated from the "merchandizing of the difference." In other words, this merchandizing becomes "the transformation into 'products,' stamped with prices and tradable in a market, of goods and practices which—under other conditions—used to remain outside the mercantile sphere."[6] Surely, so much energy would not have been invested in the inevitable return of the Spring of the Poets if this promotion of poetry did not aim at inscribing in our sensorial life the model of this merchandizing of difference. Through its circumscription of practices, sites, or attitudes in order to transform them into "cultural commodities," such merchandizing ensures their neutralization with the triumph of the reality overload.

In fact, we can imagine that a hitherto undreamed of opportunity for control is constituted by the transition of each of these "cultural commodities" from nonexistence to existence. In order to reproduce their constituent differences, each commodity must be broken down piece by piece[7] following a method that is the exact opposite of the standardization required by mass production. As a consequence, each day the merchandizing of difference encroaches a bit more upon our inner space by installing in it the reality overload of its "cultural commodities," along with the implicit aim of annihilating the strength of unreality.

And when even these merchandized products threaten to lose their appeal, because they are constantly menaced by the original contradiction of having their singularity reproduced for mercantile ends, the rationality of inconsistency soon contrives the introduction of "cycles of infatuation and disappointment"[8] in order to remedy this. Thus, this rationality more easily eclipses the magnitude of what is at stake when we are made to forget what is being lost.

In this way, we recall the refrain of the lateral critique that deplores the transformation of "cultural commodities" into so many consumer products. Unfortunately, this is not where the danger lies; on the contrary, it lies in the fact that efforts are being made to convince us that these are "different" products, thus leading us to consider them solely from an aesthetic viewpoint. This obliterates their profound meaning by abolishing the gap between them and this world of which they are the constantly reinvented depiction. It is worth noting that the enemies and proponents of cultural demagoguery are of one mind here: Both sides dissuade us from the idea that "the ruby of champagne" [Lautréamont], the "heavy ham" of dream "that hangs from the ceiling" [Reverdy], and "the ass of natural pearl" [Apollinaire] testify to a completely different reality that threatens the worlds invoked by both parties.

Nevertheless, efforts made to circumscribe in order to circumvent will never be greater than under cover of the cultural equality before us. Just as the philosophers of deconstruction have been unmasked as relativists and antiuniversalists who seek to impose their irrefutable dogmatism, so all the decoys of cultural dogmatism will have been brought into play to install a form of domination that is capable of gaining the upper hand over the realm of the imaginary. This realm's essential nature opposes the status quo. It has not been so long since this alternative offered by the imaginary still took the place of the horizon, before the rationality of inconsistency began erasing the traces of a sensorial coherence that is now disappearing day by day. This rationality of consistency is of course due to the exaggerated promise of the reality overload that now devotes its efforts to exceeding itself.

17

SENSORIAL CLIMATE CONTROL

Before too much longer, we may find ourselves blessed with a "Spring of the Realists." At least, this is what is augured by the recent investment in "reality tours" by Global Exchange, a San Francisco company "specializing in organizing trips to regions of poverty, exploitation, and conflict on our planet."[1] Global Exchange announced a million-dollar profit from a growing number of tourists visiting reality in Haiti, Cuba, Vietnam, and Ireland. This seems to be only the beginning. Based on a principle of reverse exoticism, Americans are now discovering the reality next door with the program Exploring California, which offers visits to juvenile detention centers and meetings with exploited workers or illegal immigrant laborers.

There are probably at least a few freethinkers who might call this voyeurism or recognize it as an example of a very American kind of naïveté. In fact, they—like many others who pride themselves on being above any kind of illusion—have no better vision of how their own lives are taking shape. They, too, might feel a need to turn to the reality specialists, because behind the denial-turned-loophole that authorizes most people to reject any situation that might jostle them out of their moral or intellectual comfort zone, there is no way to avoid concluding that there exists a general inadequacy to confront the reality of facts and bodies. But this inadequacy conceals itself beneath a dogmatic skepticism that replaces what is now a practically nonexistent critical thought—even encouraging the highly suspect worship of tolerance. Perhaps this is because the reality overload leads to an inability to believe in anything—or perhaps the inability to believe in anything awakens the need for the reality overload.

In itself, the information overload does not lead to an embarrassment of choices that prevents judgment, as some have suggested. It is rather the impossibility of being put back within a consistent, tangible arrangement that makes any one piece of information—whether worthless or important—seem condemned to be lost in the flow of all the rest. What's more, the uninterrupted procession of this information shuts down every perspective one by one—perspectives that until now were the natural sites in which the imagination could project itself past simple data in order to grasp a being, an event, or a situation. The collapse of art criticism, like that of literary criticism, would be unexplainable otherwise. Because of this lack of sensorial support, it hardly matters what we use as reference. Hence the plethora of scientific-seeming theories that prosper from this absence of sensibility and that have no reason to exist other than to maintain a semblance of serious-mindedness.

It follows that wherever intuition should be the primary deciding factor, we are prevented from making decisions. No doubt, the inability to judge, like the fear of being led astray, has played a large part in the infatuation over the monstrous exhibitions that are orchestrated each season and then echoed deafeningly by the media machine. We are equally afflicted by the obligatory reading that accompanies the centenary of this or that author. With respect to progress, such a reading offers an *A Rébour* (Against the Grain)* quite different from what author Huysmans had in mind. We see this most particularly in the novel's hero, Des Esseintes, who one day feels obliged to sell off his col-

*[This refers to Joris-Karl Huysmans's best-known novel, *À Rebours* (Against the Grain), which had a great influence on Oscar Wilde's book *The Picture of Dorian Gray.* —*Trans.*]

lection of Goya engravings now esteemed by others so that he will not have to experience such a "promiscuity of admiration."

There is no question that this loss of the ability to decide for oneself has become one of the goals of the cultural policy combined with the promiscuous uncertainty that now plays a role in *sensorial climate control.* Here is where suspicion tends to replace intuition far beyond the artistic realm, which has played an experimental role in this regard. Further, we cannot minimize the extent to which "the possibility of merchandising differences" contributes to the opening of "a new era of suspicion":

> While it is relatively easy to make the distinction between a crafted and a mass-produced object, between a "standardized" worker and a "free" artist, how can it be known if this thing, event, or feeling is a manifestation of life's spontaneity or the result of a premeditated process aimed at the transformation into merchandizing of an "authentic" property?[2]

How could the new frenzy to proclaim our tolerance under any circumstances have otherwise arisen? Tolerance, acting here as a virtual positivity that is capable of concealing an obsessive fear of being manipulated, not only bars emotion, but also suspends any possibility of making judgments. An example: the decade or so it has taken the international community to learn the true nature of the power exercised by Slobodan Milosevic over the former Yugoslavia. No matter how incontestable the evidence shown, the question always came back to whether we had information or disinformation. The greater the atrocity reported, the greater the suspicion it aroused, until the "ethnic cleansing" in Kosovo suddenly unleashed a flood of reactions.

Today, however, the pendulum has swung back to a much more familiar position. A consensus is forming again on the other side: Although the war was set in motion to put an end to ethnic cleansing, we are now told that the ethnic cleansing was a consequence of the war.

■

This is another effect of the rationality of inconsistency: The sensorial climate control it installs to prevent excess can lead to an excess of anxiety, which, in fact, functions as a safety device to buy time for the system to restore order. The same process can be observed in the buying fever that periodically rages in modern art museums, when the fear of missing out on some novelty becomes too great to resist. It also applies to the zigzagging, flip-flopping, and reversals of opinion exhibited by the majority of European intellectuals with respect to the Yugoslavian question. The war in Kosovo, in this regard, was a splendid remedial session for all those who, faced by evidence that could not be ignored, found themselves forced to strike another pose. What would be most instructive in this case: a calendar of the dates on which various individuals rallied to the cause of human rights—even if the delays and late arrivals were less attributable to opportunism than to a myopia resulting from the atrophying of the ability to judge.

Any display of surprise at how everything—from artistic production to crimes against humanity—has become equally unable to be judged would be most unwelcome now, and has been ever since post-Structuralist theoreticians began striving to persuade us that this was the natural order of things. In fact, adorned with all possible philosophical pomp, the new skepticism does not even have to disguise this will to deranged disembodiment—a will that authorizes all manner of audacity. Jacques Derrida affirms this same perspective without beating around the bush: "I do not believe that anything like perception exists," he says, unconsciously reinforcing Charles Fourier's idea of philosophers as those "who have a vested interest in having any problem they cannot solve viewed as insoluble."

In the same vein, this skepticism raised to the state of dogma does not differ essentially from any of the beliefs it claims to flush out in all forms of speech. Thus, it is impossible to see why we should find any more truth in the interpretation of Luce Irigaray's theory of fluids as a male chauvinist hypothesis than in the denunciation of Little Red Riding Hood as "a parable of rape" by the American neofeminist Susan Brownmiller. Neither can we see in what way the discourse that establishes their equivalence could escape this obstacle, which in reality is based on a systematic confusion between fact and fiction. This is the conundrum that many have taken great pains not to address, even though its answer would shed light on the disconcerting ease with which the theses of Holocaust deniers have taken root in both the right and the left.

In practice, we can observe just how far this can be taken with the 1984 discovery of the anti-Semitic and pro-Hitlerian past of Paul de Man, a key figure of deconstructionism. Under the pretext that "nothing is certain," his defenders, particularly Derrida, had total leeway to argue that there is no more truth than there is justice. Hence the quickly absolved "errors" of Paul de Man: It doesn't matter what we do; we are condemned to remain in the illusion of language, and if we seek to escape, we would find that the only exit buries us even deeper. It is interesting to note that Sokal's and Bricmont's fiercest opponents are de Man's defenders.

In fact, once only discourse can aspire to existence by producing "a structure of infinite returns in which nothing but traces exist" (as J. Culler teaches us in his deconstructionist doxa), it is of course difficult not to doubt everything. Likewise, paradoxically, it makes it hard not to stake everything on the reality overload from the vantage point of a process of limitless accumulation that has been pushed forward as the sole substitute available for feeling alive.

Because our property-obsessed civilization has been criticized for its consumption mania and insatiable thirst to see itself in its acquisitions, it is easy to see how this new skepticism and the reality overload are connected—heads and tails of the same coin—and what is erased is the notion of authenticity going hand in hand with the fraudulent deception of the individual and the body. This notion gained additional strength from the critique of the notion of authenticity, which deconstructionist philosophies denounced as an illusion and which was a critique developed from the metaphor of the network that made it possible to undo the resistance of both subject and meaning. This is more grist for the mill of the "connectionist" world,* which is now precipitously bringing about the disappearance of the subject while simultaneously depreciating an increasingly burdensome body.

One reason for this:

> [I]n a "connectionist world," being true to ourselves appears as rigidity; resistance to others is a refusal to connect. Truth is defined by the identicalness of the reproduction to the original—as a refusal to take into consideration the infinite variability of the individuals circulating in the network. Every time they enter into relations with other individuals, these individuals change every time in such a way that none of their avatars can be taken as the point of origin encountered by the others.[3]

Another reason: Under these conditions, the entire world must conform to the rationality of inconsistency in the face of which the body, with its minimum consistency, will always cut a figure as the embarrassing witness. Perhaps this is why we have seen such disproportionate market development for bodybuilding and for plastic surgery, which allows a person to be simultaneously old and young, to live "in real time" and not age, to run and not move forward.

Cosmetic though it may be, we must recognize a violence in plastic surgery and bodybuilding that reveals the terrible tension employed by

---

*This is "one of the principal arguments" of Luc Boltanski and Ève Chiapello's work *Le Nouvel esprit du capitalisme* [The New Spirit of Capitalism]. On page 547, the authors clearly state: "[T]he redeployment of capitalism has been associated with the recuperation of the role of the network, even though the emergence of this paradigm is the result of philosophy's autonomous history, and was at no time developed directly and intentionally in order to confront the problems that faced capitalism beginning in the 1960s."

the rationality of inconsistency to control a body that remains capable of resisting it, if only through the logic of its physical unity. There is no choice but to assume that the rationality of inconsistency is undermined by the reality overload of a deconstruction that, far from reducing the body to its functions, overstates the importance of these functions and even multiplies them—with the approval of a mob of experts who are given the task of redesigning our body image according to the whims of their constantly renewed specialties.

Whether or not it is a question of a refusal to come to terms with a problem whose end no one can predict, contesting it has not occurred to anyone. It has even become good form, with the help of skepticism, to accommodate the problem ironically if not cynically. Perhaps this is because one of the advantages of the poetic forcefeedings of which we are the beneficiaries is to offer a multitude of ersatz aesthetics to a world that has lost its imaginary horizon. These are the occasions that always find someone to mention the second or third degree [deconstructionism] with a knowing look. An interesting topic for future analysis would be the necessary vagueness of the multitude of "cultural commodities" that, like structural stopgaps, would thus be uniquely conceived to make up for any weaknesses in the production of the reality overload.

Hence the indifference that rules in the kingdom of difference, where there is no longer any question of distinguishing true from false or freedom from irresponsibility. This is no doubt why intelligence is now measured by the degree of our mental versatility—as if the turn of the past century chose to be remembered less for its delicacy than for its intellectual weightlessness. These are not at all the same, as we are taught by the rationality of inconsistency, because one of the effects of this widespread skepticism is to provoke an abundance of untimely devotions.

18

RELIGIOSITY RUNNING WILD

Because plenty of predictions have been made—with a tremor in the voice and with gauze over the eyes—that the twenty-first century will be a religious century, it is easy to see why, with the same tremor in the voice but without the gauze, these same people are far from finished bemoaning the loss of values and the crisis of the sacred. Yet when we hear today's great minds demanding a little more "discretion" on the part of Gay Pride participants, we might regret that there might also be a call for discretion concerning the pontiff's movements and other ecumenical entertainment that periodically clutter television screens worldwide. This is especially true at a time when the zenith of obscenity lies in the fact that both left-wingers and right-wingers display their joy at the pope's visit to the murderer Castro—who is himself a great jailer of homosexuals.

Religion may be in crisis, but it has not stopped traveling. And while the sense of the sacred disappears, it is surprising that our era, in its mania to celebrate what no longer exists, has not yet proposed a "museum of values" or created a "sacred space" that might coincide with certain pedestrian-only zones. Perhaps, though, we wrongly presume that religion's cultural resuscitators have total freedom of movement in a return of religiosity to the savage state.

This savagery was visible during the 1998 World Cup: Only a few days were needed in France to construct the most appalling mythology, to which was added chauvinism, multiculturalism, populism, competition, merit, and meanness—and the flames of a process of general cretinization were fanned. This rallied true believers from all countries, classes, and age groups. At least we were spared any mistaken celebration of the consensus that presided over the birth of this new vehicle of the sacred. This would have required a rhetoric in which it would have been difficult to distinguish between obscenity and profound imbecility.

Once we have gotten over the initial shock, the most impressive aspect is still how this religiosity run wild finds nourishment everywhere, rushing into any and every domain to satisfy its greed for belief. Though the disappearance of ethical benchmarks continues to inspire mourning, people have not made any effort to look at what has resulted. They are, in fact, totally blind when it comes to noting the way in which the forces in play always manage to reinvest themselves elsewhere under the most diverse and unpredictable forms.

Concerning the religious issue, it seems that the rationality of inconsistency manifests more than ever in this new arrangement. Over the last twenty years, we have seen an apparent polarization of "religious activity" in which fundamentalist groups and trends take issue with a "fluctuating religious sense": "[D]o-it-yourself logic, prevalent today in the religious sphere of Western nations, is at work inside both Christianity and those movements, where reference to a tradition is blurred by the quest for individual happiness through spirituality . . ."[1]

It is certainly possible that the dictatorship of the diverse has influenced the development of these "salad bar religions." These new modes of belief juxtapose elements borrowed from the most heterogeneous traditions, and in them, at first glance, there is clearly avoidance of any synthesis that might work against personal comfort. The growing success of Buddhism allows us to believe that it could be the object of every possible adaptation, to the point that it may be becoming *the* religion of the "connectionist" world.

Yet neither circumstantial flexibility nor do-it-yourself logic is foreign to the violence of those invoking dogmatic purity. In the fresh outbreak of religious fundamentalism we are experiencing, this fundamentalism is primarily a synthetic product onto which racism, nationalism, and terrorism have been grafted in unprecedented proportions. Because we have no possibility of knowing what such combinations hold in store for us in the future, they are similar to "genetically modified organisms."

Accordingly, despite the brouhaha the Yugoslavian catastrophe continues to inspire, its beginnings can be dated precisely to the Easter sermon in which the patriarch Paul consecrated the year 1991 to the vengeance of Serbian martyrs. The wide diffusion of this message by all Orthodox bishops corresponds to the time when it became impossible to distinguish, among the forces in play, which elements originated from the nationalist communism embodied by Slobodan Milosevic (which grew from his own personal ambitions) and which were from the ideology of a greater Serbia (the pan-Slavic sentiments of a majority of the citizens and the pan-orthodoxy of almost all of them). In 1991, when the archbishop of Croatia suggested in regard to the city of Vukovar "the entire Serbian populace must take part in the cleansing," he rediscovered, perhaps without his knowledge, the path already opened by the Serb psychoanalyst Javon Raskovic. Six months after the invasion of Croatia, Raskovic expressed his satisfaction:

> I feel personally responsible because I laid the groundwork for this war, although it did not involve military preparations. If I had not incited the emotional tension within the Serbian people, nothing would have happened. My party and I set the match to Serbian nationalism, not only in Croatia but everywhere else, Bosnia-Herzegovina especially. We led these people by giving them their identity.[2]

Having said this, Raskovic did not neglect to reveal the secret of his success: "Human reality is enriched by the destruction of inner worlds. The ethical reality of the Serbian people has been revealed by cataclysms."[3]

The key is undoubtedly this "destruction of inner worlds" that allows all possible and imaginable products of synthesis to replace religion. This brings to mind the reutilization of waste products, most notably in the realm of food, where many of us are aware of the problems reuse has caused in the existence of mad cow disease and that have been caused by the release of dioxins. Many things that have previously been identified as harmful or at least questionable surface again in the form of hitherto unseen heterogeneous mixtures. Indeed, even in the fabrication of "politically correct" ideology, we see the systematic reuse of the very conservative forces whose effects the partisans of this ideology claim to be fighting. We can note in this ideology the same mendacious moralizing, formalism, and strictness—and though these undoubtedly blend with ingredients from the new economic order, the ideology still responds to the same need to believe in order to avoid actually living.

Yet it would be a mistake to limit the field of this false conscience to the embodiment of what is politically correct. Today, incredible tolerance is granted to intolerance. In fact, under the pretext of respecting beliefs in all their diversity, freethinkers and atheists are tolerated on condition that they keep their mouths shut. Attacking religion is now viewed as both out of place and out of style. Woe to whoever dares recall the limitless villainy used to justify the different creeds. Anything that cannot be consumed becomes disturbing compost in which the most astonishing forms of religiosity proliferate. We are at the antipodes of the healthy ecology practiced by Minsky, the Ogre of the Apennines, whose profession of faith Sade happily recounts in his book *Juliette:* "I eat everything I fuck." Going to the diametrically opposite side, we find God, who, with the help of the reality overload, has less and less trouble governing from atop his throne of accumulated wastes. Chased out of the front door, he has been allowed to sneak in through the back by the sudden interest in spiritual thinkers. It is not propriety that has kept the left wing from proceeding to an intersection of Trotsky and Péguy. We have the "genetically modified" thoughts we deserve.

It is true, though, that devotion to principles never seems to check a practice dominated by the skepticism with which our new era can justify all its failings. As Benjamin Constant pointed out long ago: "Fools make a compact, indivisible mass out of their morality, so that it interferes as little as possible with their actions and leaves them free in every detail."

One of the essential aspects of contemporary devotion is to manifest an enthusiasm inversely proportional to the reality of the relationship maintained with the object of that devotion. This can be seen today in the way believers in surrealism are torn between the castoffs of the young combat veteran and those of the old Boy Scout who has lost his poetic troop. Situationism acquits itself no better, having become in the space of a few years the credo of the prevailing cynicism. This has reached such an extreme that the major thesis of situationism is invalidated: The thing has been replaced not by its image, but by its opposite. This has been done so skillfully and to such an extreme that emphasizing the spectacle would no doubt constitute the best means for diverting attention from how the harnessing of meaning is now perpetrated on a broad scale.

This harnessing is made possible by the growing pressure of the reality overload, which now short-circuits all discourse and even prevents it from assuming the slightest magnitude. Perhaps this endemic religiosity is confused with an illusory quest for a distance that is increasingly absent from both the way we exercise our thought and the way we perceive our body. Equally besieged by the reality overload, both our thought and our body are condemned to return to the greater triumph of insignificance, through the reciprocal reflection of their solitary confinement. We are witnessing the advent of a time of ideas without bodies and bodies without ideas.

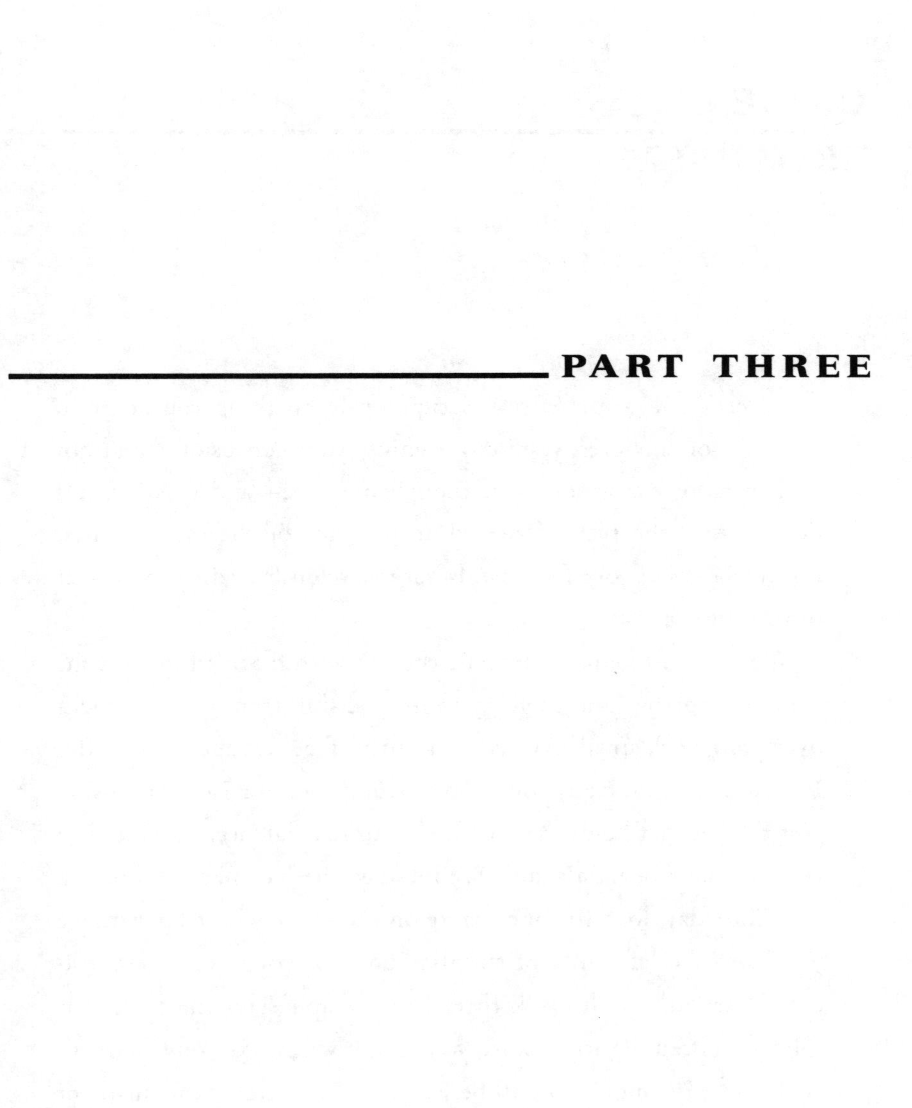

PART THREE

19

UNISEX EROTICISM

My pretty one, your passion scrupulously breaking you apart in pieces before my eyes, yesterday evening, your confusion could not be any more victorious, even though unaware—and this is but a detail—that the play of the white patience of the one hundred knucklebones of your foot stands out marvelously against the velour of your intestines.

Would you like us to arrange the hat with black tulips of your womb tomorrow, and then try to lift the skin from your buttocks over your back until it veils your entire face, except your smile? It would then be ready for Sunday afternoon. For Monday, I suggest the hat that holds the double of your natural face. For Tuesday: the hat made of hands, and Wednesday, the hat made of breasts. For Thursday, we will concentrate on the shape whose appearance you love: the left wing of the iliac bone of your pelvis, embroidered carefully with black thread that emphasizes the surface it follows. Tilted slightly toward your ear, it will make you beautiful. As for me, I wonder if I will be wearing the stretch pants made of your seamless legs, decorated along the inside with pieces of faux excrement.

Once I find myself benumbed beneath the pleated skirt of all your fingers and weary from undoing the garlands with which you have encircled the somnolence of your unborn fruit, then you will breathe into me your fragrance and your fever, so that in full light my sex will emerge from yours.[1]

Between this love letter imagined by Hans Bellmer in 1957 and everything fobbed off today as erotica, there exists the same divergence that separates the recent installation of "First Arts" at the Louvre—containing sculptures in all their splendor from Africa, Asia, Oceania, and America—from the dreadful sculpture that was exhibited one hundred yards away in the Palais Royale during the spring of 2000 (as if Buren's columns were not enough).*

Did I say divergence? Neither distance in space—which is nonexistent for Bellmer and hardly the ends of the earth for "First Arts"—nor distance in time, fifty years for the former, one to ten centuries for the latter, can begin to convey an idea of the abyss that now exists between almost all the products of contemporary expression and an entirely different kind of consciousness. To me, this consciousness seems to manifest dissimilarly but from the same necessity in realms completely foreign to each other in appearance.

There will be those who will be shocked at this comparison of an erotic tradition exemplified by Sade, Pierre Louÿs, Georges Bataille, and so forth and the immemorial sculptures whose poetic charge—beyond any and all interpretation—has been created from the benchmarks of the sublime.

Should it prove impossible, however, to compare the circumstances surrounding their respective appearances, I would still not hesitate to recognize the same poetic awareness at work in both. I feel authorized to do so by Apollinaire, who was simultaneously the inventor of the *Masters of Love,* the "sole person truly to concern himself with this important question"[2] (as Robert Desnos stressed in 1923), and the first to describe himself, in *Zone* ten years earlier, as being so tired of "living in Greek

*[The columns, created by the French sculptor Daniel Buren, are contemporary, black-and-white columns of various heights that were installed in 1986 at the traditional-looking Palais Royal. —*Ed.*]

and Roman antiquity" that he wished to return to: "Sleep among [his] fetishes of Oceania and New Guinea."

There is a similar affirmation of continuity in the perception and reproduction that give form to mystery in both the deepest burrows of amorous singularity and the remotest reaches of collective awareness, whether these perceptions and reproductions were conceived in the secrecy of personal solitude or in that of initiation.

This is all the more evident when we note that primitive societies, when confronting life's essential moments, offer each individual the possibility of taking the universe as his or her witness and finding an echo there for otherwise inexpressible concerns. In contrast, Western tradition does all it can to work against such an aspiration to stake everything on the interpenetration of the physical and mental worlds. This heightened awareness can be obtained only at the cost of a sensorial heresy, renewed at distant intervals, for which just a few individuals have not been scared to pay the price. The insurgent history of true poetry is testimony to this, but its course would not have the magnificence of unpredictable colors or improbable moves if the erotic path had not crisscrossed it continuously.

Thanks to Jean-Jacques Pauvert for the gift of his irreplaceable *Anthologie historique des lectures érotiques* [Historical Anthology of Erotic Readings], we know how to discover in what way—often underground—this sometimes secret and always parallel erotic path has meandered through time as an indestructible means of "winning back lost powers." Irregular, sinuous, and perilous, with vertiginous ascents and astonishing descents, this path appears no less than the privileged one that thought has used to return in order to confront the obsessive unreality of the body.

As Pierre Louÿs states in his famous preface to *Aphrodite:* "Sensuality is the mysterious yet necessary and creative condition for intellectual development. Those who have not felt to the limit the requirements of the flesh—whether to curse them or love them—are thereby incapable of understanding the full extent of the mind's requirements." By itself, this observation shows just how much the origins of philosophical libertinism at the beginnings of the seventeenth century reveal that the conquest of freedom of thought is indistinguishable from that of freedom of morals. A century later, the Encyclopedists* were far from achieving this level of freedom of thought in quest of itself, the price for which was the ruin of Théophile [de Viau], even after he was acquitted in 1628.† In addition, Claude Lepetit, author of *Le Bordel des Muses* [The Brothel of the Muses], was strangled and burned in 1662 after having his right hand cut off. In the eighteenth century, Sade alone invoked this twin heritage of libertine thought, but he paid for it with thirty years of prison time. Because of this, he will never be forgiven, just as he will never be forgiven for having introduced philosophy into the bedroom, whereas today the only concern of well-meaning individuals is to keep the bedroom in philosophy.

From this power of displacement—and no one brought it to its peak as skillfully as Sade—the erotic path evidences the rare ability to help us climb back to the tumultuous source of thought, where it becomes one with the inner illuminated desire of the functioning of our own sensibility.

It is for this reason that I stress the importance of *La Petite Anatomie de l'image, petite anatomie de l'inconscient physique ou l'anatomie de l'image* [The Little Anatomy of the Physical Unconscious or the Anatomy of the Image]. In this book, Hans Bellmer succeeds in extricating several laws of the "anatomy of love" from an overall view of this "physical imagination" through which "the body can formulate in its own language against the natural order to which it is subject." Outstanding among these laws is that "any given detail, such as a leg, is perceptible, accessible to memory, and available (in short, is real) only

*[The Encyclopedists were a group of eighteenth-century French philosophers who collaborated, under the direction of Denis Diderot, to produce the Encyclopédie. —*Ed.*]

†[Théophile de Viau (1590–1626), a poet and essayist, was condemned for his views as a libertine, homosexual, and Protestant. —*Ed.*]

if desire does not fatally take it for a leg. The object identical to itself remains devoid of reality."[3]

It would be hard to conceive of a more radical antidote for the reality overload that today is thrust upon us from all sides. What's more, this secret of love, which is also the secret of poetry, according to which "the object identical to itself remains devoid of reality," is perhaps the last weapon we have at our disposal against a world in which individuals and things are increasingly forced to remain identical to themselves. Individuals and things must also provide insulation against anything that is otherwise—as proof of their identity—which, as we have seen, requires the affirmation of all difference. This text by Bellmer remains unheeded and seems destined to stay that way—perhaps because its lightning flashes illuminate certain abysses of the amorous night.

It is in this sense that the recent appearance of an alleged erotic novelty, which in the last two or three years has become a mandatory ingredient of all fiction, seems to prolong in veiling, even if this novelty is presented as an unveiling and an unprecedented liberation. In fact, it does not occur to anyone to denounce the relentless persistence with which what was once kept hidden is now revealed, or to repudiate the frenzied desire to distribute on a mass scale what was once an intentional rarity. This has been done in such a way that it is now impossible to harbor any doubts about the triumph of the reality overload.

All things considered, there is no reason for sexuality to be spared this treatment. We have only to consider the diligence of today's novelists in filling some sort of sexual quota by striving to name this or that sex organ as many times as possible. The banality of the expression is meant to serve as the guarantor of its strength. We come away from these books with the disagreeable impression that sex is somehow put back in its place—even as the texts attempt to present it as the belle of the ball.

The equivocal nature of this attempt is pushed further. The writing that literary critics attributed to young novelists, who primarily desired avoiding lyricism and other nonsense under the pretext of restoring the body to its physical truth, actually came from a very different origin. In fact, the honor for such writing goes to a platoon of female novelists who, in a charmingly housewifely way, with the help of postfeminism, took the erotic question and put it into an unexpected order. This order was increasingly muscle-bound. We can still read, in an early feminine novel entitled *Meat:* "The orgasm is ecstatic nausea. Ecstasy, metastasis, fucking rubbish, *fuck you.* Always the big words."[4] Since that time, the minimalist determination of these female novelists' young successors has arrived to reinforce the effects of the use of sex that such women writers standardized in their work.

The truth is that this sorry conversion of amorous territory was first explored by newly emancipated women writers, from Benoîte Groult to Hélène Cixous, who paved the way for the following generations (from Françoise Rey to Marie Darieussecq)—women who were even more emancipated. These later arrivals cheerfully rushed in the wake of those first authors to rejoin them at the antipodes of what Rimbaud had in mind when he wrote his famous letter of May 15, 1871, to Paul Demeny:

> When the infinite servitude of woman is broken, when she lives for and by herself because man—hitherto abominable—has given woman her release, she, too, will be a poet! Woman will discover the unknown! Is her world of ideas different from our own? She will find strange unfathomable, repellent, delicious things; we will take them, we will understand them.

■

Alas, nothing strange, unfathomable, delicious, or even repellent has resulted from this brisk unveiling. It has only provided a kind of sexual version of the standard banal novelistic impoverishment, but its intensive production—to each his truism—seems beyond anyone's capability to stop.

We can believe that there is nothing surprising about the fact that people follow in the footsteps of others—as long as we do not read enough of these books to discover that, from one novel to the next, as if in the same novel, bodies meet, the same or different sexes couple, and all couples follow, one after another, with the same lack of differentiation. Paradoxically, this is the consequence of a reality overload of fluids, stickiness, tumescence, swellings, and discharges that cover with one glutinous layer the most dismal unisex eroticism.

And even while language watered down to infantile levels coexists with a rhetorical vulgarity taken to scatological extremes—yet another example of the rationality of inconsistency—this unisex eroticism still displays both hedonistic and Miserabilist colors. These hues manifest in both the ritzy neighborhoods and the slums, and this eroticism nonetheless always obeys the same sex-realism that nobody seems to consider abandoning.

It also hardly matters whether the author is a man or a woman, heterosexual or homosexual, lesbian or gay. These texts are as interchangeable as the characters inhabiting them—people who leave no memorable impression of a body, a face, or a sex. But judge for yourself:

> When I came, I leaned forward, burying my organ further down her throat at the moment I ejaculated. Alice uttered a smothered moan—my prick was gagging her—and her eyes suddenly opened wide in panic, while my sperm was sliding down her throat.
>
> And:
>
> Then I brought him into the bedroom, where I fucked him first from the front then from behind. This took a long time, and it was really quite nice. I pushed in and out, his ass making a very loud flotch, flotch, flotch noise. He groaned as he crouched beneath me. I began to get soft because he was too large.

And:

> For her—more than anything in the world, she liked to have her ass fucked, and her pussy. She pulled me closer, clutching me tight. She gave a few thrusts with her pelvis, crushing her breasts against me. I started off—my heart followed suit. She moaned—in pleasure. Bitch, she thought we were done. No way. I gave her a smack.

And:

> I put a finger up her ass. She put one up mine. Above us, the flooring creaked. We bit each other's lips. I pulled her breasts from out of her bra. Her nipples were as firm as rubber. I grabbed her ankles and spread her legs apart in a Y. Her vulva seemed to spring off its hinges. I spit on it and moistened it with my palm. She dug her nails into my buttocks. I liked that. I turned her over. She plunged her hand between her thighs and blindly played with both our sexual organs. Mine. Hers. Both at once.

Examples such as these go on and on. It appears superfluous to provide the names of the authors of these lines. Suffice it to say they are between the ages of twenty and fifty and male, female, or even representatives of the third, fourth, and fifth sex. They should, however, reassure us of the pleasures we have in store from this new erotic creativity that is destined to spawn itself indefinitely in similar cut-and-paste, all-purpose texts.

Because our era excels in its discernment, many who do not know how to read proudly exclaim that Sade is boring—yet they do not perceive that the sexes and bodies he shows us constantly are always more eloquent than the most skilled psychological analysis. He presents Juliette in full when he writes, on introducing her: "She had the whitest ass and the blackest soul." The same holds true for Walter, the anonymous author of *My Secret Life,** who evokes just one out of some twelve hundred women "of twenty seven different empires, kingdoms or countries, and eighty or more different nationalities, including all those in Europe except a Laplander." He depicts little Jenny as lying

> still as death. . . . The light fell full on her backside; I could see a lightish brown hair in the crack of the parting of her buttocks, a smear of shit on her chemise. Her flesh was beautifully white. She had on nice white stockings and flashy garters.

The diary of this Victorian gentleman covering a period of some forty years clearly proves that quantity plays no part. Obsessed like no other, Walter is not a Don Juan so much as a specialist. Yet, attentive to the storms of desire, he looks and looks at the other to see born there the vertiginous space of an inner turmoil that belongs no more to him than it does to the other.

Walter's example is a far cry from our industrious contemporary authors, who certainly have not been prevented from getting erections, ejaculating, and "having it off"—but without the evocation of any unease or the improbability that can give the act of love its irreducible singularity.

It is as if this new fiction illustrates, through the genital specialization that characterizes it, both the "localization" and that "contraction of the libido [in which] the erotic is limited to sexual experience and satisfaction,"[5] as Herbert Marcuse evokes. He presents the notion of "repressive desublimation" to explain a "pseudoliberation" that "works for, rather than against, the status quo of general repression."[6] This desublimation is practiced "from a 'position of strength' on the part of society, which can afford to grant more than before because its interests

*[Banned for one hundred years for being too obscene and pornographic, *My Secret Life: Diary of a Victorian Gentleman,* by Walter, is now considered a historic and erotic masterpiece. —*Ed.*]

have become the innermost drives of its citizens, and because the joys which it grants promote social cohesion and contentment."[7]

We cannot help but note how well this analysis provides advance corroboration of the characteristics of the "new spirit of capitalism," in particular its new "vocation . . . to market desire, especially that of liberation, and by that fact, it recuperates and frames it."[8] Marcuse does not hesitate to speak about "institutionalized desublimation," to the extent that by "diminishing erotic and intensifying sexual energy, the technological reality limits the scope of sublimation"—so much so that "the tension between that which is desired and that which is permitted seems considerably lowered"[9] to reach a point at which "satisfaction [is achieved] in a way that generates submission."[10]

Because of this, it does not appear aberrant to recognize in this repressive desublimation, and in the antagonistic forces it sets in motion, a crucible in which the rationality of inconsistency can grow. Marcuse explicitly states: "The way in which controlled desublimation may weaken the instinctive revolt against the established Reality Principle can be illuminated by the contrast between the representation of sexuality in classical and romantic literature and in our contemporary literature."[11] In fact, to the extent that sexuality appears "absolute, uncompromising, unconditional" in works such as Racine's *Phèdre,* Goethe's *Elective Affinities,* and Baudelaire's *Les Fleurs du mal*—works in which "it is beyond good and evil, beyond social morality," and beyond the reach of "the established Reality Principle"—in contemporary literature, it is expressed in a way "that is infinitely more realistic, daring, uninhibited. It is part and parcel of the society in which it happens but never as its negation."[12]

More than thirty years ago, Marcuse was already emphasizing that "this society turns everything it touches into a potential source of progress *and* exploitation, of drudgery *and* satisfaction, of freedom *and* oppression. Sexuality is no exception."[13] Nevertheless, he could not foresee the importance sexuality would be given, nor what a strong example this sexuality would set, increasingly circumscribed from itself and prohibited from any passion-based perspective.

We can only recall the relentless perseverance displayed since that time—especially over the last ten years—by philosophers, novelists, essayists, filmmakers, psychologists, psychoanalysts, journalists, and specialists on every subject. These individuals combined their efforts to discredit amorous passion, which they leave to the innocent if not to the simpleminded. In hindsight, this begs the question of whether all of these individuals haven't taken upon themselves the task of making us conform to the ideal of the "connectionist man," this "entrepreneur of himself"[14] who practices "a kind of self-monitoring"[15] to be "a connector," "a transporter,"[16] and by virtue of this is careful to avoid any profound bond that would impede his "flexibility." It could even be presumed that the current vogue for a certain neolibertinism is *the* amorous theory of the connected type, for we know this type deems it especially important not "to become enclosed within preestablished bonds in order to remain available to try new connections that might otherwise come to naught."[17] In this "connectionist" world, the "large is only as *light* as its freedom from its own values and passions."[18] There is no question of seeking a balance between passion and connection.

No doubt, not everyone has the facility to "reinvent love," as desired by Rimbaud. But no one can say that amorous passion has nothing to do with eroticism and pornography. From the "white straddling of panicked women" to the "sleeper with dampened hands," the entire opus of Pierre Louÿs testifies otherwise, as do the works of Apollinaire, Joë Bousquet, and so on. It is clearly understood that "eroticism is an individual science. Each resolves according to his worth the secondary questions and finds agreement with his peers only in acknowledgment of the insoluble nature of the eternal questions whose existence we never tire of proclaiming."[19]

■

These are questions that our era seems to have settled, as we can see from an expert on all mediums such as Catherine Breillat with *The Book of Pleasures.* The sole interest of this text is as an anthology of pages that, as its author informs us, "took possession of me. I was no longer in my normal state of mind."[20] In fact, this interesting anthology establishes in thundering fashion how the reality overload and repressive desublimation now combine their effects of confusion, redundancy, and inflation in more ways than one to install the incomparable vulgarity of this new *eroticism of proximity.* Initially, we can cast no doubt on the objectivity of this anthology, even if its objectivity is due only to the distressing impression of uniformity it leaves in the mind of the reader. It is not enough that a certain number of authors from the past have been taken hostage in order to allow for the erotic impoverishment of contemporary authors. If we find Patrick Besson and the Marquis de Sade, Pascal Bruckner and Lautréamont, Cyril Collard and Rabelais, Jean-Luc Godard and André Hardellet presented in this dismaying hodgepodge as the "supreme orgy," it is because all of these authors have been uniformly reduced to illustrations of a set of themes worthy of a computer menu: "The Sexes," "The Couple," "Pleasure and Virgins," "The Pleasure of Debasement." The indigence of these themes is covered over by drum-roll commentaries that are an equal mix of pomposity and the ridiculous. A few examples are enough to impart an idea of this: "Desire is a virtual object that has every appearance of reality."[21] "Physical love is the equivalent of extinguishing death. It's the leper's kiss."[22] "To write about pleasure is to discharge in the body of the reader."[23]

By itself, we could view this theme as "a nonnegligible quantity of no importance"—if this anthology was not a part of the growing din surrounding sexuality, a chorus regularly echoed by all the weeklies. In other words, we could view it this way if the erotic bludgeoning did not correspond to already familiar poetic bludgeoning—resulting in the same framing effects, effects that seem to bring about a grandiose short-circuiting of sensibility, which this time seeks to score a hit upon its physical origin. Never before has it been possible to assess to this extent how much the reality overload tends to become confused with a *censorship by excess.**

All leads us to believe that this pillaging of the erotic aims not only at the destruction of the erotic, but also at its disappearance as the source of any form of representation. In the absence of the erotic, following the model of this unisex eroticism in which representation disappears under a flood of copies of the same, we witness a complete collapse of representation in a wide variety of domains. Now by ceding to the reality overload, does representation have any other possibilities except to founder in endless reproduction?

*The corresponding phenomenon in the information field is what Ignacio Ramonet calls "democratic censorship" in *La Tyrannie de l'information* [The Tyranny of Information] (Paris: Galilée, 1999), 39.

20

S/M, OR SEXUAL ROLE-PLAYING

Luckily, we have philosophers—feminist to boot—to show us the way. In 1986, Élisabeth Badinter, obviously enthralled by her discovery, declared at the end of an exposition entitled "L'Un est l'autre" [The One Is the Other]: "Our mutant hearts no longer seek the pangs of desire. It could almost be said that there is no other choice. The model of resemblance exists in conjunction with the eradication of desire."[1]

Luckily we followed this exhortation. Today it has earned us the ability simultaneously to experience the triumph of sadomasochism (S/M), the return of Charles Péguy,* the entrance into service of the National Library of France, genetic manipulations becoming commonplace, and the proliferation of serial killers. There are so many figures of the same celebrated so warmly by Élisabeth Badinter that in one burst she sacrifices desire (already on the road to eradication) in this exhortation, as well as passion, which is not the promise of a more radiant future, because "passion is on the road to extinction, sensual vertigo, too."[2]

It hardly matters now that since 1986, through a bit of hocus-pocus on the part of the rationality of inconsistency, the same has become the enemy of the good. The affirmation of difference has made it possible to put the same and the other back to back, as if they were nasty

*[Charles Péguy (1873–1914) was a noted French poet, essayist, and editor. —*Ed.*]

killjoys, but at the same time invite them to come in again through the wide open doors of identity.

The fact remains that despite this, neither the critiques of the same nor the effacement of the other has been abandoned. It would even seem that both are encouraged on condition that they go no further—in other words, on condition that they continue to perform the role of screen for this "eradication of desire" that in the final analysis haunts the problematic of the same and the other, but about which people customary remain silent. Only Élisabeth Badinter's impatience broke this silence and thoughtlessly formulated what was revealed to be the priority of priorities.

If this is not the case, how do we explain why no one has picked up on the monstrous nature of this "eradication of desire" that makes up the concluding argument in Badinter's book in which such great store has been set. Even if this argument was possible, to overlook the increasingly virulent morality it uses brings all the equivocal elements of the rationality of inconsistency into play. In the name of multiculturalism, everyone seeks and finds his hopelessly uncultivated roots. In the name of openness to the spirit of universalism, tourism is devastating the planet. And in the name of the equality of the sexes, sexuality is pushed back into its place. Examples of this relegation go far beyond the confines of literature, which now serves at the whim of a hygiene-inspired destitution. This has been demonstrated over the last few years by columns on practical sexuality that can be found in all the women's magazines, not to mention the new male-media approach to sexual issues, which are treated by this medium with the same seriousness—but less lyricism—as new car features.

Of course, the function of unisex eroticism is to give rhythm and color to this endeavor of forcing desire to toe the line, like a voice offstage that sets the tone. Furthermore, its lack of a decisive scope is tied to this vocation of damage control. It is from this vantage point that the predominance and the perseverance of the S/M style are particularly enlightening, especially when we are explicitly told what S/M is and what it is not, as a certain "Juicy Lucy" has done on behalf of a group of American sadomasochistic lesbian feminists:

> Here is a list of things S/M is not: abuse, rape, hitting, violence, cruelty, power over another, force, coercion, nonconsensual, unimportant, a choice made lightly, growth-blocking, boring. On the other hand, S/M is: passionate, erotic, fulfilling, consensual, sometimes fearful, exorcism, reclamation, joyful, intense, boundary-breaking, trust-building, loving, unbelievably great sex, often hilariously funny, creative, spiritual, integrating, a development of inner power as strength.[3]

This is not a joke, but an image that is becoming increasingly widespread: In the United States and Europe, everything that gave sadomasochism its specificity until quite recently—from pain to humiliation—has been cunningly toned down. After all, why should S/M have any better chance of escaping this reduction than salmon, cosmetics, or any other cultural commodity from a universal system of fraudulent naming? In any event, its actors, books, and testimonies combine to confirm the same notion of an S/M that is more impressive due to its paraphernalia than to its insignificant rituals.

There seems no need to mention what we can recall from Sade (of course), Sacher-Masoch, Bataille, Arthur Adamov in *L'Aveu* [The Confession], and from Blaise Cendrars in *Emmène-moi au bout du monde* [Take Me to the Ends of the Earth]: They make inconceivable a masochism in which the individual does not seek to lose himself, even beyond pain, in a dizzying spiral of degradation.

Perhaps things have changed, but what is called S/M today has nothing in common with the spaces of devastated consciousness in which sadism and masochism once took on meaning in an eternal half-light of frenzy and trembling. The gap is so great that again we can perceive how many different and divergent gestures, behaviors, and attitudes the same words describe—and so well that it is impossible to write off as an oddity from across the sea what gave us, for example, Annick Foucault's *Françoise maîtresse* [Mistress Françoise].

By all evidence, the great success this autobiographical work has enjoyed since it was printed in 1994 can be explained as a reflection of increasingly widespread practices. But this success can also be attributed to the fact that the text clearly exposes this distressing novelty: "All of this is theater and theater is not reality. It is not a question of breaking an individual either physically or psychologically. To the contrary, it is necessary to play at being bad in order not to be bad."[4]

It could not be any more explicit. What we have here is sexuality finally reduced to a role-playing game and, what's more, a socially useful role-playing game.

On top of this, Annick Foucault explicitly states in an interview: "I believe that we human beings need to be allowed to show a certain weakness. If this weakness is theatricalized, if it is acted out, what's the problem? We come back from our experience strengthened, swapping our chains for three-piece suits, and we return home soothed and fortified."* We are struck by the closeness of her position and that of her famous namesake Michel Foucault, who claimed that S/M is not "a reproduction, within an erotic relationship, of the power structure. It is a reenactment of power structures through a strategic game capable of producing physical or sexual pleasure."[5]

It will be noted that in any case, the cost of this theatricalization has been a manifest desexualization, if not an implicit elimination of the erotic from the moment S/M "basically decided to play power games,"[6] as Léo Bersani points out.

This is not inconsequential; such a slip from the erotic stage to a theatricalized simulacrum of power relations deactivates what connects

---

**L'Événement du jeudi,* May 19, 1994, quoted by Jean-Jacques Pauvent, who, for his part, emphasizes the strangeness of S/M with respect to the sadomasochist tradition in his introduction to Annick Foucault's *Françoise maîtresse,* 7.

the actors to both the story and their own bodies. This therefore allows us to see that the reality overload paradoxically finds nourishment in this reduplicated derealization, if only through the overabundance of harness rigs and accessories used to disguise the erasure of the individual body held hostage by what is also a theater of nondifferentiation. Even the oppressive repetition of the same scenes, the same services, the same reenactments in the S/M trend of current fictional productions confirms a similar intention to have done with the body through the inflation of practices that allegedly celebrate it.

In this sense, S/M constitutes the best example of censorship through excess. We can even be inclined to view it as equivalent to one of those "loops of recuperation" with which "the new spirit of capitalism" leads certain forms of freedom to establish "new oppressive mechanisms."[7] Topping this, Michel Foucault, who desires to disengage S/M from any politics relying on the use of force, "seems to suggest that the sadomasochistic pleasure results from the insertion of the master-slave relationship into the framework of a game, but it is not inherent within this relationship." In other words, "domination and submission become sources of pleasure only when they are made aesthetic, chosen as simple conventions to permit the game to take on concrete form."[8] It is hard not to see in this a slightly more sophisticated variation of the morality that compels Annick Foucault to introduce and then justify S/M as a socially beneficial practice.

We have reached a point where we may wonder if the increase in the sales of corsets, masks, boots, chains, whips, handcuffs, and harnesses might not be directly proportional to the progress of a morality that these outfits also serve to mask. This morality already guarantees, through S/M and its completely controlled practices, the disappearance of the sexed body and the formidable routing of trouble-making desire, which, in the final analysis, seems to be the main business of our time.

All that everywhere else is an act of flaying
Here is but a beautiful and chaste disrobing

All that everywhere else is an undermining
Here is but a solid and long-lasting sloughing

No, this is not the latest stage of an unpublished S/M poem, but four lines from Charles Péguy's *Cinq prières dans la cathédrale de Chartres* [Five Prayers in Chartres Cathedral].[9]

Yet it is easy to mistake it for an S/M poem; the morose moralizing and repetitious rhythm of these weighty litanies have much in common with the redundancies of S/M, as well as with the desexualization in which S/M participates and which is being established slowly but surely in our time. This desexualization is so widespread that it is hard for me to credit chance with the renewed attention given to Charles Péguy over the last decade.

As antimodern as his principal rediscoverers (from Jean Bastiaire to Alain Finkielkraut) pretend to be, their fascination with Péguy's nonpoetry—which sinks ever deeper into the glebe of the real—appears as most contemporary at a time when the incapacity for soaring flight has become the best pledge of nonsuperficiality. And would it be justified to raise questions about a rebellious thought in the categories where one has sought to billet it? I cannot force myself to disregard its strength as an ontological shackle, condemning everyone to labor indefinitely in the fields of reality, independent of the fact that everything takes place, as in *Françoise maîtresse,* beneath the harsh dominatrix gaze of the Virgin Mary.

As for the "carnal country" whose lost secret some seek in this philosophy, it makes me shudder—especially when I consider the matter through which this fascinating "enfleshment" is summoned to manifest. Earth, stone, wood, and even flesh on occasion—it doesn't matter, but this should be primarily "serious matter" whose essential characteristic is that it is definitively asexual. Further, it must be asexual to the point where all is desexualized, even "the sins of the flesh and not of the flesh":

The terrestrial sins
The earthly sins
The muddy sins
The sins of the glebe
And the terrestrial earth.

This is a fine example of enfleshment in which the flesh is cruelly lacking. This is why there is no need to believe in sin in order to be disabled by this insistent repetitious expression that has no regard for the other, which is just good enough to be convincing, and which does not appear to be so different from rap as we might think. Without overemphasizing matters, I would not hesitate to claim that the effacing of the body that these litanies describe triumphantly has everything necessary to seduce an era in which the same lost body is responsible for styles such as piercing, branding, scarification, and tattoos.

Far from turning us away from religious masochism, this growing appetite for body markings is the paradoxical expression of a similar denial of the body that is tolerated as the support material for everything it is not. While it is true that "prison tattooing is a significant indication of personal resistance to the loss of identity induced by incarceration that subjects both time and body to constant investigation by guards,"[10] it seems that something totally different is at work here. This style marks the body less to give it singularity than to remove its erotic nature—to signify a decentering that changes everything: Here is the specific element at the origin of desire, erased for the benefit of a symbol that testifies to a difference, but a difference shared with others—indeed, with an entire generation.

It would be convenient simply to view this body marking as one of the more illusory methods of regaining control over a body that no one is very sure what to do with. But it is also another way of putting sexuality back in its place. It hardly matters that these different body markings help proclaim membership in some sort of community or that they inscribe the trace of something that has no symbolic power other than this inscription, when the body is brought back to itself by these alterations that dissuade it from venturing toward the other and reinforce it through narcissistic redundancy. What's more, what we see reemerging here, decked out with all the prestige of modernity, is the vast, age-old suspicion of the body, which is reiterated daily under the pretext of sexual liberation, brought up-to-date by S/M, aestheticized by markings, and obviously reinforced by every variety of religious expression.

Further, this body, which we are still naive enough to think is our own, after it has been a metaphor for the world, for thought, for desire—how can it now, prevented from being a metaphor for anything at all, avoid being the extra body that is such a just cause for alarm? This is so not only because by being "placed into parentheses by daily life, the body comes to an individual's attention in the form of a symptom."[11] Nor because by being mechanized and mediated, its relationship to the world tends toward becoming nonexistent. And not even because the representation of the "connectionist" man associated with the image of the network quite simply dispenses with the body.

Certainly, all of this contributes to the terrible threat of a humanity that already dreams of being bodiless. Most alarming, however, is that day after day we are losing the means of resisting this threat, when—as Élisabeth Badinter announces and advocates—there is occurring the catastrophe of a passionless human being and a sex life that consists of assembling "because we look alike and want to see the same reality in the same way."[12]

From coupling to reduplicating, the best means of making us forget that the amorous body has been and remains independent of all styles and centuries is that it is our sole means of transport. The least merit of unisex eroticism will not be its successful reduction of desire to convivial cloning.

21

CORPOREAL ILLITERACY AND GENETICALLY MODIFIED LEARNING

By a paradox capable of shedding light long after it has ceased being a source of surprise, Mallarmé, regarded as one of the greatest crafters of language, who dreamed of The Book* his entire life, invented the idea of *corporeal writing.* One evening in 1886, the movements of La Cornalba,† who danced "as if unclothed," prompted him to declare:

> The dancer *is not a woman* who dances for these combined reasons: She is *not a woman*, but a metaphor who sums up one of the elementary aspects of our form, sword, cup, flower, etc. And that *she does not dance* suggests, through myriad short-cuts and leaps, with a corporeal writing what it would take paragraphs of prose, in dialogue and description, to express: a poem set free from every implement of the scribe.

Mallarmé's last great poem, *Un Coup de dés* [A Roll of the Dice],

*[The Book was a concept that Stéphane Mallarmé worked on for thirty years. It was a cosmic text-architecture: a flexible structure that would contain "all existing relations between everything." —*Ed.*]

†[La Cornalba was a ballerina. In his writing Mallarmé often used the dance as metaphor. —*Ed.*]

made visible the importance of space with respect to the movement and development of his "naked thought" on the page. This notion of corporeal writing appears far richer than that which has aspired to analyze gestures and behaviors like letters, without ever truly taking into account the space in which they are deployed. Paradoxically, it is through its physical subtlety, at the antipodes of all semiology, that this corporeal writing helps us envision the corporeal illiteracy that is the foundation for the spectacle we see in the streets today.

There is no need to consider at length the comings and goings of passersby in order to ascertain that their movements, seemingly indifferent to the space in which they occur, stem from the most rudimentary body language. But what could they have to say, these human bodies that seem convinced that they are free as long as they resemble one another, even as they disappear beneath a plethora of T-shirts and sweatshirts that reduces them to an undifferentiated mass which can only transport whatever is written on their clothing?

The only reason these human bodies move this way would seem to be to display the brand name of what counterfeits them so well, in the literal as well as the figurative sense. Often added to or substituted for this brand name is a text that serves to deny the identity of whoever is wearing the piece of clothing. We have only to consider the infinite selection of T-shirts that immediately transform the wearer into someone sporting a sandwich board and providing advertising for cigarettes, radio stations, or—like a joke—the wearer, but stating words that are not his or her own.

Interestingly, the higher we climb in the social hierarchy, the more discreet the text, until it is reduced to initials that are recognized only by those who are initiates of quality. Those who are illiterate wear Columbia University sweaters, those in upper management dress like hoodlums, and professors cultivate a three-day beard that makes them look like fugitives from justice—and they do this in order to feel at ease with themselves by pretending to be someone else.

Of course, other people are in the streets wearing stretch pants and Lycra. These are skintight and restrict the body in order to contain it within the limits of a specific athletic or erotic role that denies its infinite possibilities.

In addition, with this corporeal writing it is possible to see how greatly contemporary indigence is dependant upon a body reduced to an increasingly worn-out presence. Indeed, corporeal illiteracy should be just as alarming as the illiteracy we all believe has been exhaustively defined. Further, if it has proved impossible to halt the galloping progress of the latter, why should we be concerned about the former?

It is true that people have been less concerned about the apparently less alarming misuse of words—undoubtedly, because it is a focus of those who consider themselves to be the literati. Yet while we can surely gain an interesting picture of the way we live by indulging in lists of the faulty translations and misinterpretations that increasingly enamel contemporary language, we can nevertheless still boil down this illiteracy to placing the standard dictionary side by side with a dictionary of approximation. It is as if, for want of finding a way to be embodied and echoed through a corporeal writing, language is suddenly condemned to spin its wheels in approximation. This, at least, is the impression that professional writers, journalists, reporters, and presenters of all kinds give—and these people, obliged to use the most common words, seem to cling ever more tightly to redundancy as if was a life preserver.

Thus we can hear them striving to "join forces," to "soldier on" in the secret hope of "finding unanimous agreement" in order to prompt "common communion" or to forestall any potential "collective mass psychosis," if not to "foresee it in advance." In this way they hope to ward off what they are each day a little less capable of perceiving as an impoverishment of language—and at the same time, they reinforce these impoverishing effects by reducing each word by adding one or two synonyms to it.

That we are not more concerned by the insignificant nature of increasingly similar bodies testifies not to a particular disinterest in language, but rather to the significance of even the most ordinary exchanges that are the sole innovation of this particular fin de siècle [end of the twentieth century]: *pleonasm** as a mode of thought giving structure to and perpetuating the reality overload. As a result, imitation has become the basis of a representational system that exhausts itself in claims of its novelty.

From this vantage point, the resounding failure of the National Library of France† constitutes a spectacular success. If failed actions always proclaim a truth we want to hide, the defective realization of this library that is meant to resemble no other also reveals its essentially redundant nature.

In their desire to achieve the announced plan of a completely digitized library, the heads of this edifice were forced to reconsider the existence of the concrete works overlooked in their initial considerations. In order to avoid giving the impression of abandoning their plan to digitize their complete collection, the library heads were forced to transfer onto magnetic tape a large number of books readily available in the framework of a traditional library. What was exposed unintentionally in this aborted project was the kind of technological intimidation that previously had hidden successfully behind the promise of universal access to "all the learning of the world." What had been introduced as "an entirely new kind of library" was, in reality, only a monstrous pleonasm.

To tell the truth, many should have foreseen this from the overall architectural conception of the library. Organized around an empty esplanade of fifteen acres flanked by four corner towers shaped like

*[*pleonasm* = the use of more words than necessary to denote mere sense. —*Ed.*]

†[The new, enormous Bibliothèque nationale de France was built on the outskirts of Paris during the first half of the 1990s. Most users must pay a fee to use the library. Its architectural design, location, and user-friendliness have been the subject of controversy. —*Ed.*]

"open books" set some three hundred yards apart, it implied an endless series of both essential and useless comings and goings, as has been verified since then by the unfortunate users condemned to trek several miles, even if simply looking for a book.

Still, those who spread the story of the library remained strangely cautious and minimized the scope of the disaster. Most stopped with saying it had "the feeling of a catastrophe that has already occurred—a disaster against which nothing could be done and which we would have to put up with while striving to make it right through ingenuity, patience, and resourcefulness."[1] It is as if the bluff of the novelty of the computer continued to conceal the indigent principle behind this gigantic duplicating machine. Meanwhile, a growing pile of grievances came from the readers who allowed themselves to be snared in this labyrinth of redundancy. These complaints concern the repeated control procedures to which library visitors are subjected while they are perpetually obliged to keep moving, and the huge number of files that send users back and forth repeatedly, after which they are told that the book they want does not exist—even though they can provide the book's date and place of publication.

So much tolerance for so much inconvenience would remain inexplicable were it not for the fascination of the end of the twentieth century for a cloning venture leading from the same to the same. The architect of this library, Dominique Perrault, revealed his reasons, which would have caused another era less enamored with redundancy to shudder: "To create a building closed in upon itself gives more autonomy." We cannot be surprised, then, that under these conditions, "the entire edifice—reading rooms with artificial light, steel towers with escalators, steel rooms for the photocopiers and toilets . . . brings to mind a prison."[2]

Nor can we be surprised that, now condemned once and for all to follow well-marked routes that forbid any hope of discovery, readers can verify, through simple comparison to the previous national library, that the fatal effect of pleonasm is not to create an identical reproduction, but rather to erode and debase what it is supposed to at least confirm, if not improve.

This is why I cannot attribute to chance the fact that the sharpest criticisms of this "Very Great Library" (this was the name of the initial project) occurred *at the same time* that farmers first rebelled against the patenting of life that aimed at "imposing, then taking over, the transgenic seed market." In this process, seeds are always identical but are usable only once, in order to "abolish farmers' time-honored practice"[3] of saving seed and then reseeding their crops every season.

Likewise, from another perspective, it is possible that any indulgence toward this "Very Great Library" is encouraged by an analogy between the book of all knowledge, which this library is supposed to be, and the Book of Man (our DNA), with its wealth of some three billion chemical symbols, which genetic biology offers us today. In both cases, the illusion of mastering the whole rests on rendering all its elements equivalent. This is a technical illusion if there ever was one, but it lies at the origin of a similar acritical attitude embodied by these "new races of researchers who, according to one of them, Daniel Cohen, are no longer satisfied with traditional methods but instead want a technobiological revolution" that "introduces productivity into research."[4]

Duplicating what already exists or reducing it to an infinite number of identical elements tragically amounts to the same thing. Of course, it is the best way of introducing productivity into the most varied fields, along with providing the bonus of the constitutive positivity of redundancy, indiscriminately developing into idealism, moralism, or hygienism like so many ways of shoring up the reality overload. Further, while the "DNA truck drivers and roadmen," the "marathoners of the genome," don't allow any doubt about this, the promoters of culture are not resting on their laurels. We can see this in the operation launched in February 2000 by the RATP (again) and the Louvre, offering "travelers the chance to discover through the eyes of contemporary artists the works exhibited at the Louvre."

Thus, in the name of aesthetics, emotion, and cultural animation, the redundant gaze of these artists is thrust upon us. They not only achieve the tour de force of making completely interchangeable a painting by Le Sueur, a drawing by Watteau, and a study by Delacroix, but they also succeed in making all of them identically meaningless.

Didier Lockwood, jazz violinist and composer, says this about the Valentin de Boulogne painting *Concert au bas-relief,* in which three figures are depicted, one of whom is a musician at a table: "[T]his painting reveals the convivial nature of music. Music is an art around which people gather. Here, around a table, people play, another reads, another is drinking . . ." This powerfully penetrating commentary rivals that of Aziz "of the Orchestra National de Barbès," who describes Eustache Le Sueur's *Terpsichore:* "[I]t is the generosity of music but also its strength. Look at the woman's posture, how straight she is holding herself! Look at the movement of her arm, which is lifted to hold her instrument."

Best of all these observations is that of Daniel Humair, who, contemplating the study of an Arab lute by Delacroix, exclaims: "If you hung this painting in a gallery today, nobody would think it was a Delacroix! You would imagine it to be the recent work of a contemporary artist." Is it because Daniel Humair is both a "musician and artist" that he earns the right to unveil the aim of the operation: that any artwork can be the product of any person and any time? In this way, he renders the work equivalent to itself, after first having caught it in the snare of the promiscuity of pleonasm.

This is also the snare of the networks in which, as Pierre Lévy explains, "the human being, his language, and his world are engaged in a circular coproduction."[5] Indeed, we cannot doubt this, in light of the joint RATP-Louvre announcement that the exhibit they sponsored "must be renewed two or three times a year based on different themes," and that in the meantime, commentary on "poetic works will follow in the footsteps" of the art commentary.

We cannot help but see that this art-commentary operation involves the development of aspects of our heritage never before exploited in this way. That this kind of exhibition might have serious consequences for our heritage seems to be no obstacle to the will "to take apart this monstrous puzzle" and "break" it into a thousand pieces, as the geneticist Daniel Cohen says.[6] And even if "the works remain in the museum," the project known as "A Ticket for the Louvre" works to destroy the singularity of the works in order "to permeate the most unexpected moments of daily life." We can only hope that this idea is restricted to the metaphorical plane. Meanwhile, regarding the National Library of France, if we are to believe the report of Inspector General Poirot ("breakdowns followed one upon the other, the shelving units jumped their tracks . . . books fell" such that "every incident could prohibit the communication of the works to the readers"[7]), then the risk of the physical destruction of the books is all the more real given that the problems concerning their storage and distribution, as the same report tells us, "stem from the poor quality design of this shelving."

The fact remains that resorting to the same managerial language to use in talking about realities as distant from each other as the book, the cell, and a work of art displays the extent at which a certain violent process is imposing its redundant order on the sources of both thought and life—under the same pretext of "assistance."

In this regard, we can pursue comparison between the "linguists of the genome"—who, before the gene was sequenced, sought to "position" genes between two chromosome "beacons" that served as reference points for a "localization" preceding "identification"—and the new geneticists of the written word, to whom the National Library of France offers its novelties. The titles of some of the features offered by this library form an entire program on their own: For example, the PLAO (*postes de lecture assistée par ordinateurs*—i.e., computer-aided reading stations) permit the researcher "to work with the document . . . annotating it, underlining it, establishing reading paths, etc." And the PABN (*postes d'accès à la bibliothèque numérique*—i.e., digital library access points) offer the reader the possibility of accessing "the sociological [and] historical environment" of the text he or she is consulting, or in other words to follow the "reading paths" others have prepared for the library patron.

We need not be great scholars to deduce that this machine has been designed to produce an infinite number of commentaries that are given more importance than the original text, which is now reduced to the status of a supporting role. And it does not take a genius to notice that this "new temple of knowledge" is not merely a machine that functions for the sake of functioning, with the sole purpose of exalting the emptiness around which it is organized, like the majority of contemporary accomplishments. Monstrous as the library may appear, it is nonetheless quite emblematic of a world in which, if we can still believe its head aficionado, Pierre Lévy, "the Web predicts and gradually achieves the unification of all texts into one lone hypertext, the fusion of all authors into one sole, collective, multiple, and contradictory author. There is no longer anything but one text: the human text."[8]

Sometimes stupidity has the charm of truth. Here, it points out the parallel disappearance of otherness and negativity. The flow that achieves this also produces and feeds the National Library of France as well as cultural promotion, whose mode of functioning seems only to reflect itself. But concealed in this promotion is a mechanism of chain-linked substitutions, which remind us of the series of substitutions that give us genetically modified organisms.

No doubt, others have noticed, over the course of the last few years, the catastrophic manner in which hypertext, intertext, and pretext have succeeded in obfuscating the idea held by certain naive individuals from the time of the book, which served as a unique, public object in which thoughts are inscribed to become grounds for exchanges or confrontations. But, thanks to the new modes of reading promised by the National Library of France, it seems we have moved on to a higher stage. These new ways incite researchers only to look for commentaries and data that can be substituted for the text in order to benefit an orgy of interventions that are all supposedly equally valid. They are certainly not equal because they are of equal quality. Their equality stems from the fact that all of them, like so many variations of the same, are developed on the model of pleonasm, with all the falsification that this implies, and they grow worse with each additional rereading. This should bring joy to future pedagogues, particularly to two members of the French Association of French Teachers, who would like to do away with the literature "of dead authors, or those well on the road to becoming dead." Their preference is for "a universe of signs, riddled with references and endless rewrites."[9]

Pursuing the genetic analogy, we can see here the equivalent of manipulations intended to "improve" the functioning of our thought and produce a *transgenic knowledge*. Likewise, it could be said that we are witnessing a gigantic grooming of reading in which the most vague kind of learning, based on accumulation and juxtaposition, is substituted for actual knowledge of the texts.

This knowledge manipulation is something that was neither anticipated nor denounced during the polemics and controversies that attended and followed the building of this matchless library. As Jean-Marc Mandosio notes, "[E]ven today, although everyone can see the failure, no one dares draw the obvious conclusions." He also points out that "the objective pursued was not the computerization of a library" but "rather the construction of a whole new data processing system intended to supplant the library by substituting itself, eventually forcing the disappearance of the library after having rendered it totally obsolete."[10] In other words, this "new temple of knowledge" is in fact the temple of a new learning whose intent is to destroy the book it brandishes as the pretext for its construction.

This deception and planned destruction is so obvious that it is dumbfounding to see how many people continue to believe it to be simply an isolated phenomenon. Meanwhile, the achievement of this project is emblematic of the same pretensions of an era that is also active in both genetic and cultural engineering. In fact, this deception has become so obvious that we can hardly miss signs that the same danger is emerging from the fact that the symbolic unity of the book is threatened by the same process of substitution that threatens the genome.

Data processing encourages infinite succession, and we have become accustomed to it as the way of the world, but what it really involves is a new process that knows no limits—a process used by the reality overload to proliferate at the heart of everything that exists. This proliferation affects even the way we imagine and perceive crime—which can be attested to by the supremacy that we accord serial killers. Just as the new National Library of France shows that its sole reason to exist resides in "its overall organization that encourages flow and scorns the reader,"[11] so the current prestige of the serial murderer shows that he or she loses all identity beside the reality overload of the quantity of his victims, who are too numerous to be given any sort of individual identity. We prefer the crime of the same over the news item that favors the individual, the detail, the specific circumstances. Yet why should not the reality overload have its own crimes, just as it has its own eroticism, now that both have joined forces in the great project of the "eradication of desire"?

22

EDUCATED VANDALISM AND BODYBUILDING

Every spring we have the burning cars, the drag races in parking lots, the demolished bus shelters, and the damaged phone booths to remind us of the existence of the suburbs and, at the same time, of a new form of vandalism that has no dearth of sociologists and psychologists to study it. And fortunately, this suburban vandalism draws attention away from the other end of the spectrum: the degradation brought about by diploma-holders, which now threatens all cultural objects. Nothing is spared—not the book, as we have just seen, or the monuments and historical sites that are now at grave risk of being restored.

Surely, there is far less need to work at preserving the hideousness of large apartment complexes and the everyday ugliness of vehicles—each of which is like a million others—than to bustle about, for example, attempting to restore the keep of Falaise, "one of the most important twelfth-century dwellings in Europe," of which "the little that remains visible inside the medieval structure is . . . completely invaded by modern intrusion."[1] As for repairing the Grotto of the Pines in Fontainebleau, whose decoration has been entirely reinvented "based on a few indecipherable fragments,"[2] this is hardly a matter of "social debate." We cannot expect anything different regarding Château de Chamerolles,[3] an authentic Gothic manor in Loiret that was transformed into a fake Renaissance château following the intervention of an architect of historical monuments.

Apparently, there's vandalism and then there's vandalism. The difference lies in the limited nature of uneducated vandalism—the kind that attacks Les Minguettes and Courneuve* and their adjacent supermarkets—and the educated vandalism that aims at a larger target in time and space.

It would be too easy to stop here. If any sort of literary criticism still existed, perhaps our intellectual observers would cease to view as an enigma what they happily describe as the flooding of the novel by eroticism (a phenomenon we discussed earlier). Perhaps they would be able to discern that the body, now offered to us as a free gift with the consumption of every novel, has no reason to envy the fate of historic monuments that are renovated in their restoration—not to mention the fate in store for the book.

In addition, in France, there is a strange coincidence between the timing of a new policy concerning French national heritage and the appearance, in the 1990s, of products and boutiques devoted to body care. This might be viewed as a simple confluence of circumstances if we could not also note a coincidence between the recasting of the past as put into practice by this new architectural restoration and the present picture offered to us by this so-called renewal of the erotic. This notion of the erotic is itself inseparable from today's generalized notion of bodybuilding.

For a decade now, bodybuilding has no longer been the prerogative of only the cretins who opt for muscular hypertrophy (just as people once upon a time chose mortification of the flesh). Today, people are bodybuilders in the same way that they drive cars—that is, without taking note of the fact. Now and then they are sculptors or anatomists of their body in the same way a car owner sometimes takes on the role of car mechanic or engineer. Furthermore, through the rationality of

*[Parisian suburbs. —*Trans.*]

inconsistency, this driver, who more and more acts as if he has no legs, is often the same person as the bodybuilder, who strives to rediscover, among other things, the use of his legs. In both cases, people maintain the same distance from their body, viewing it as merely an accessory. (The driver regards the body as a burden, and the bodybuilder regards it as a source of gratification.) It hardly matters that the bodybuilder might as well be working tirelessly to transform his body into a mass of hubcaps. Where the reality overload rules, the accessory has no destiny other than to serve as a substitute for the essential. Thus, subjected to constant tune-ups in weight-lifting rooms and relentlessly maintained at a state of optimal functioning by the appropriate nutritional chemistry, this accessory body becomes the double that embodies the famous "self monitoring"[4] to which the "connectionist" aspires.

When treated like the other that must be mastered or even vanquished, the body finds itself to be the material as well as the starting point for the reconstruction of a runaway identity. Like a pleonasm of muscles, pursued constantly by repetitious exercises and a regular training regimen, and always on the verge of being revised and corrected, this body is confirmed as the most reliable synthetic identity. Simultaneously a fortress, a carapace, and a muscle combination, this synthesized body imposes itself as the preeminent integrated identity. This identity, however, results as much from the erasure of the original body as from the erasure of the sexual body, and can be no more than providing ourselves with armor plate against other people.

Yet all kinds of relationships between body and machine—the body as machine, the body as the extension of the machine, the body induced by the machine—have long been imagined. With the technological development that makes them increasingly achievable, we forget that the true danger lies in the monstrous redundancy of useless muscles or prostheses that are more tempting than they are necessary. The resulting reality overload results in a process of adulteration that nothing can interrupt—not even anorexia, whose alarming rise is in keeping with a desperate resistance to this excess of bodies.

▪

Thus it is not at all disorienting to hear Bruno Decaris, the head architect who restored Château Falaise in the purest blockhouse style (judging by the criticisms that followed), bragging about having given "the fortress its primary quality as a building of war." He takes "credit" for burying against the front-entry facade of the great keep a vanguard of gray cement embellished with various metal elements. He says that a castle keep "should be impressive, it should cause fear. . . . This is not an architecture of tenderness but of violence."[5]

This "restoration" amounts to not only claiming pleonasm as an intervening principle, but also proudly exhibiting it—like the bodybuilder displaying his musculature. In this instance, we are providing for the concrete existence of a "small entry castle," which seems to have no reason for its presence save as a reduplication of the main keep. What's more, the same occurs both in the field of restoration and in the contemporary novel, in which the deliberate accumulation of every sexual platitude is viewed as a sign of modernity—which leads to the reconstitution of an erotic body that would be more at home in a book on anatomy. In restoration, an ostentatious demand for pleonasm has the value of an "architectural gesture," thereby authorizing all manner of indeterminate substitutions. This denies the very nature of the monument, gradually transforming it from a historic place to historical commonplace that conforms to cultural authorities' ideas of not merely preserving a place, but also "developing" it.

Beyond the obvious concern for profitability, which is inseparable from a cultural policy that has inspired "the birth of a two-speed heritage: one to which waves of public money flow and the other condemned to destruction or slow death,"* we have good reason to remain alert to the resulting *formatting*. Of course, this is in line with what has been

*This was deplored as early as 1994 by several art historians in the first issue of the review *Momus,* in which they have since continued their critical activity.

put into practice regarding promotional poetry, but here it also has a bearing on time and space. As for the reconstitution of the erotic body, taken to an extreme during the summer of 1999 by mediocre women novelists from whom women's magazines commissioned articles: We can regard it as the extension of this same formatting taken to the individual sphere—and, of course, going hand in hand with a boom in plastic surgery.

We can pursue this comparison further, including the positive perspective in which we have come to view these recent forms of ingenuity. Whether in matters of the restoration of historic monuments or of human appearance, the goal of "improving" always supplies the excuse for any intervention. Miserabilistic as the evocations of the new fictional eroticism may be, it never alludes to any kind of amorous desperation. The only negative idea that can be introduced is the "breakdown"—but this is introduced only for advancing the story, because the machine is quickly put back in working order, even if it functions solely for itself. It is important only that it functions and can thereby deny any sign of aging or exhaustion. This is the objective of all the men's and women's magazines that now print erotic maintenance columns. They offer as a standard solution an array of behaviors that are each more stimulating than the next.

The rationality of inconsistency does balance the picture with risky activities such as bungee jumping, mountain climbing, trekking, rafting, and survival ordeals. But by directing outward the quest for physical limits, these activities aim at giving us the confidence that brings us back to ourselves. In all likelihood, this is because "where sense is absent, the senses pick up the relay and allow physical experience of a world that appears to be stealing away symbolically"[6]—but also because this new practice of controlled risk reinforces a narcissistic withdrawal, which is on its way to becoming the norm.

In fact, from bodybuilding to these examples of risk-taking, there is only a question of "self-referencing," to use a dreadful neologism, which describes perfectly the feverish pleonasm that governs these activities. In addition, covering ourselves in muscles and collecting risks stem from the same frenzy to concentrate upon ourselves all the signs of contemporary positivism—even if it means caging ourselves in a cockpit of good conscience in which it is easy for every trace of individuality to disappear.

Furthermore, the constant rise of risks reiterates the positive value of an adventure that has been rationalized just as we have rationalized weight-lifting rooms. Like bodybuilders constructing their body, neoadventurers construct their adventure, but not without relying on technical expertise that is as discordant with the areas to which they travel as the body is with the various apparatuses intended to remodel it. Because

> . . . the neoadventurer is an entrepreneur, the risks he takes are far from being disinterested and chancy. Independent of the sincerity of those who experience an adventure and the dangers they invite to confront them, the adventure thus consecrated is now a flourishing industry, a source of publicity for the industries that finance it. Thereby it gleans a symbolic legitimacy, manna for the media, a new motif for stardom, and the creation of countless jobs . . .[7]

As an expression of the rationality of inconsistency as well as the logic of the network, something that ought to lead away from civilization returns instead right to its heart—and that which should escape functional tyranny ends up feeding its motor forces. The body as adventurer triumphs today only because it is able to serve as a pretext for this return of positivism to itself; but it triumphs like an overrated actor in a contrived plot, demonstrating the reality overload of the bad theater of our time.

I therefore cannot resist the temptation to make a comparison to the same functional positivism that seems to have prevailed through what has been dubbed the "white and gold vandalism," which appeared with the "years of the patrimony."[8] A simple analysis of the characteristics of this positivism suffices to make its noxious nature visible.

> Instead of maintaining and repairing the monument that wears its history like wrinkles on a face, there are a great many operations, more or less rash, to make the monument correspond to ambiguous data from old documents and ancient depictions. These are unclear and vague, [but along with hewing to them, we make the monument hew to] the preconceived idea the architects have of it today, or to the branding desired by its underwriters. This adulteration affects every element, from the basic structure to the monument's facings, from its dormer windows to its decorative moldings.[9]

Thus, under the pretext of restoration, destruction takes place. The historical white elephant, chosen in a vague fashion, hinders the recovery of the integrity that the addition is supposed to restore. Such renovation has almost reached the point at which we are destroying constructively, as noted with some consternation by the historian C. Edson Armi in his "Report on the Destruction of Romanesque Architecture in Burgundy." We are discussing the world on the other side of these archaeological reinterpretations, the world in which "preservation is viewed as simplistic historicism, and invented reconstruction is seen as pluralism."[10]

Sadly, the situation concerning nudity is no different. Nudity is decomposed, recomposed, exhibited, but is tragically absent from all the denuded bodies offered to us. Though these bodies conform less to standard canons of beauty than to those required by the various athletic, sexual, or relational roles they are supposed to fill, there is not one of them that expresses desire for the other.

"Alone, she will never be completely nude," Radovan Ivsic wrote in 1941, revealing the secret of nudity illuminated in a desire for convulsion without which neither passion nor love exists. This is a secret that has apparently been lost, given the countless nudes that are not nudes and demonstrated by the variety of monumental hybrids that result from the same adulteration.

Indeed, how could it not be necessary to destroy bodies and their symbolic extensions in order to arrive, through heavy reliance on physical performance and chemical prostheses, at the constant re-creation of bodies sheathed in doubles that make them prisoners of themselves? Similarly, isn't it from the fact that they owe their expressive strength to the combined effect of time and form that historic monuments and sites have become the object of this crusade of reconstructive destruction? And the cultural policies of left or right would not compete to promote the destruction if an unprecedented muddying of sensibility wasn't at work through them, dispossessing us of our feeling for the authenticity of things and places, as well as our perception of the material nature through which is revealed their unique character.

In this way, the adulteration of monuments is comparable to the adulteration of the erotic—and both, whether through the architectural edifice or the amorous body, set their sights on the form taken by the unique.

23

CONCRETE DEMATERIALIZATION

Here, I can disappoint all the inattentive moralists—from neofeminists and Christian and Muslim fundamentalists, to those obsessive detectors of reification and the progressive representatives of a virtue that is always offended, to those who believe they can point to perfect examples of the various strategies of the reality overload in the flourishing market of pornography—from X-rated films, videos, and CDs to books and albums for collectors.

In vain I have studied a considerable quantity of these pornographic products to use as an illustration of the adulteration I've been discussing. As the action of an order that systematically adulterates itself in order to impose itself, this adulteration is always cultural. But in pornography, we have bodies coupling for the sake of coupling and offering the spectacle of their coitus to whomever takes pleasure in viewing it. Those fools who think themselves cultured can continue to strive uselessly to distinguish eroticism from pornography by transforming into aesthetics all aspects of it that they find frightening. It is precisely to get away from these cultured few that pornography remains a reserved realm—one that is traditionally the purview of a specialization that is proclaimed and displayed in the books and films that are presented as the catalog of a thousand and one images from an exclusively sexual world.

Certainly, there are more gratifying voyages than those proposed by the pleasure industry, whose commerce has grown from what was once quite small and clandestine. Though often barely elaborated, the paths of the pleasure industry always lead to the reverie that continuously opens into a hidden doorway for deserting reality. Because it has been fortunately displaced, this world of X-rated films and publications runs alongside our own, like our world's playful double in which only a sexual end can be envisioned for every situation. Like greedy children imagining a world of chocolate houses and caramel streets, where everything can be licked, sucked, or eaten, those who use pornography avail themselves of enchanted worlds where the realization of desire precedes its formulation. Finally, the excessive nature of copulations—in which the only reason the vulva does not fill the entire screen is to leave room for a wider shot of the diagonal assault of the vulva by the phallus—gives this world the prestige of unreality and, even more strangely, the prestige of passion-based unreality.

Against this variation of the fairy tale—which is often insufficient, but in which pleasure, facility, and often laughter combine to abolish time in the immediacy of embarrassment—reality opposes the normalized space of run-of-the-mill novelists. In their novels, the undercover trivialization of sexual activity is used as a master trump to erect a dam against lyricism, with all its implications of tangible indigence and the impossibility of love. What passion should we use as our authority when everything is relative? What's more, if lyricism draws so much of its strength from being one of the rare vehicles of warding off death by virtue of producing the sharpest awareness of the effect of time on the physical body—unique because it is mortal—we can then perceive the dispossession that threatens us. Through the growing opportunities it offers us each day, this new erotic banality gives us the possibility to unlearn how to distinguish between the similar and the unique.

This major dispossession is hard to evoke in all realms where it deprives us of the emotion that is inspired by the original instead of the copy. If true enthusiasts can recognize this emotion and are rarely deceived, it is hard to believe that others can be totally ignorant of it.

Until recently, the unique character of an object was perceived, whether by varying degrees or unconsciously. In architecture, this characteristic has always drawn its strength of expression from an unconscious perception by establishing how much the building reconstructs the surrounding space. In the best cases, it creates a unique place. From one era to the next, the popular fondness for certain places, going beyond their hazy historical resonance, also testifies to this perception, which has become a standard for distinguishing true from false.

This may be stating the obvious, but revisiting this point was quite useful to the late art dealer Daniel Wildenstein, when he was disturbed by the practice of advance buying of paintings that were not yet painted. Speaking out against the "visits and discoveries" of museums on computers today, he recalls that for him, "there is only *one* way to understand and *one* way to love a painting: that is by seeing it." He goes on to say:

> I first entered the cave of Lascaux, the real one, the good one. And I was enchanted. It would be hard not to be. It is extraordinary how well time and beauty go together. Then afterward I went in the other cave—I entered the copy—but this one had no pedagogical value. No beauty. No sense. The copy is nothing. It is null. They are attempting to make us believe the opposite, obviously, but this gimmick has about as much value as Bill Gates' little images. . . . You sit down and look. What do you look at? Nothing.[1]

Unfortunately, the reality has grown worse—for it is not simply *nothing,* but something else entirely that we are supposed to look at . . . something deriving from the disappearance of the witness coupled with Hobson's choice.*

Perhaps we can look once again at contemporary practices regarding

*[Hobson's choice is a free choice in which only one option is offered and one may refuse to take it. The choice therefore becomes take that option or don't take it. —*Ed.*]

the preservation of historical monuments. Such preservation is increasingly characterized by brand-new paint, the addition of molded pieces of stylish accessories, and, most often, as at Fontevraud Abbey, "an inextricable play of new hybridizations of the successive historical eras, of homogenous and combined restorations of these different strata, and contemporary inventions."[2] Thus we can recognize the multiple aspects of a single effort to erase tangible landmarks, leading us to forget the meaning that the original building—even ruined—still carried. It is as if the reality overload of the deliberate additions was meant to assert itself to the detriment of the ruin's reality—and to do so to such a point that we might call it *concrete dematerialization*.

Disturbingly, it is far too easy to make the same observations about the shape taken by, in both life and fiction, the contemporary reconstruction of the body. Whether the contemporary novel relies on realist intimidation to impose its crude perceptions or relies on various forms of surgical, chemical, or dietetic tinkering (which give the strength of law to the norms of a corporeal design that is no longer hampered by any kind of singularity), it is easy to note how the grafting of artificial elements is essential to ensuring the triumph of the reality overload. In this case, the reality overload puts the finishing touches on its adulteration of the body through its hybridization.

From this we can even conclude, with regard to monuments of the past and the body of the present, that there would not be such an intense attempt to convince us of their materiality if materiality was not precisely the missing element.

This concrete dematerialization constitutes the progressive loss of all tangible relationship to the world, thus prompting the acceptance of the ruses of this dematerialization in order to gain an impression of living. More than ever, the object of the attention and pressures of the reality overload—namely, the body—remains the threatened substitute of a relationship to a failing world. Long ago, Novalis declared: "The body is the necessary organ of the world." For want of acting as this organ today, perhaps it is becoming the most cumbersome of prostheses.

We have reached a point where, by comparison, Lichtenberg's knife* without a blade and handle has taken on an aura of authenticity. Its total immateriality gives it a coherence that cannot be claimed by any body or, as we have seen, any of the places and sites that have recently been restored. Doubly dispossessed, these places no longer exist except through the loss of their material integrity and through having been stripped once and for all of the imaginary integrity they maintained in the state of ruin or reverie.

So there are no grounds for believing chance to be responsible for this concrete dematerialization as one of the most disturbing manifestations of the reality overload. Even greater support for this premise can be found in the fact that this excess of reality seems to have found its theoreticians in 1990 during the historically prominent "Heritage Discussions":

> It was clearly necessary for the wings of dream to begin beating again, for the ruin to become an emotional symbol again, and for the ambition to bring a building back to concrete life to reappear. In the final years of the twentieth century, accompanying Disneyland's arrival in Europe, a presage or syndrome of a new taste, a kind of restoration-reproduction-re-creation experienced a boom that recalled the glory days of Viollet-le-Duc.[3]

■

Since that time, there have been a multiplicity of projects to improve certain sites, such as the Brocéliande Forest, threatened with being rigged out with a "Grail Castle," and Auvers-sur-Oise, where, "due to the most modern and sophisticated techniques (ambience provided by soundtrack, the most faithful reproduction of the decor, projection of images onto unusual surfaces, special effects, etc.), the visitor will be able to dive back into the time of the Impressionists."[4] These projects reveal

*[Georg Christoph Lichtenberg's description of an impossible existence was "a knife without a handle and a blade." —*Ed.*]

the ridiculous extent of the efforts made by a determination to occupy every bit of space, as well as to monopolize all eyes and ears with these substitutes, in order to prevent any outburst from the imagination.

Further, concerning historical edifices, the anachronism of the restoration is not necessarily appropriate, while historical clichés most often fill in for the real restoration. Recourse to a technology of facsimile always leaves an impression of concrete substance: we might even say concrete brutality, on which all cultural ingenuity today is wagered, from the promoters of amusement parks and the architects of historical monuments to the favored artistic expressions of "performance art" and installation.

Even on its own, the term *installation* indicates the weight of the reality overload governing this kind of undertaking. There is not a single museum that hasn't paid sacrifice to this effort—with a disarming consistency of repetition. We can even note that a work's value is directly proportional to its concrete brutality. The success of Christo's monstrous wrappings certainly doesn't contradict this. Neither do Ousmane Sow's realistically ugly mastodons from the spring of 1999, which attracted such large hordes of Parisians who were so stunned by the weight of that art that their own weight threatened to collapse the pont des Arts.

As for the performance art that constitutes the other extreme of contemporary art, a reference borrowed from the world of sports describes exactly what it hinges on: At the junction of an ethos of competition and a practice of productivity, the artist is the hothouse hero who produces himself. A hybrid of the sportsman and the neoadventurer, his only value is to mimic the process of concrete dematerialization that incorporates all his activity.

Last, when it comes to brutality, we can look to what governs the most contemporary art of all: photography, at least in its most evolved incarnation. Though it no longer strictly imitates reality with all its defects—something Baudelaire held against it—it is dismaying to see that the majority of photographers appropriate rather than imitate the work of their predecessors, adding to it in a way that is equal parts vulgarity and pretension.

The great photographers of the human body were the first to be afflicted by this practice, which is equivalent to architecture's restoration-reproduction-re-creation, which embraces almost all cultural activity. In this way, Man Ray, Bellmer, and Molinier paid the price for similar embezzlements, whose creators are among the most famous of contemporary artists. These artists are due recognition for killing two birds with one stone. What we find in their work is that the human body and its representation reciprocally trap each other in the snare of the reality overload.

The worldwide success of Disneyland shows that this takeover by force is well on the way to succeeding. Not only our personal relationship to time and space is manipulated here. What finds itself petrified is our age-old power to deny both time and space in the name of the marvelous. Reducing the world of fairy tales to a banal, three-dimensional reality is a tragedy comparable to the devastation of the huge forests. This is why it is not enough to bemoan this paving over of the marvelous without taking stock of the consequences. If the world's oxygen supply is dependent upon the size of its forests, and if the devastation of the mental forest is equivalent to the devastation of the actual forests, what dream will still give us sustenance when we find ourselves invited to witness the actual forests' systematic destruction?

We can reckon less and less with historical monuments: The addition of elements that possess only a vague relationship to the whole eventually destroys the sensorial whole these monuments continue to form, even in a ruined state. This is the point when concrete dematerialization, paradoxically reiterated with the construction of these hybrids, rises up as a bulwark against the imagination.

In fact, because they are neither false nor authentic, these revised, corrected historic monuments have complete license to impose themselves by the substitutive mass of what they are not—until they completely obstruct the imaginary perspective. Lacking reference to any tangible event, their solid presence rarely fails to inspire a new kind of bewilderment. This bewilderment is inevitably reminiscent of that engendered by the nonplaces of excessive modernism: airports, parking lots, commercial complexes, and so forth, although it is from their reality overload, empty of any meaning beyond their casual roles, that these constructions draw their power to confound. In them we have monuments whose characteristic is to deny the human body the implicit reference of every spatial construction—the body that was long "conceived as a portion of space with its frontiers, vital centers, defenses and weaknesses, strong points and defects."[5] Here, monuments reflect only a single functionality and by definition conceal the physical and psychic integrity of their users. Despite appearances, the same is true for so-called historic monuments where, with all their substitutions, the temporal dimension as a concretion of individual and collective life is conjured away, and where the concrete dematerialization of what had created profound meaning ends up producing places reduced to the status of empty decor.

It should not be surprising, then, that the emergence of the discourse on the famous "places of memory" that, as Pierre Nora says, allegedly speak "to our contemporaries about who they are by showing them who they are no longer" has coincided with the multiplication of these historically pretentious nonplaces. By manhandling the awareness of times past as well as that of current events, such places deceive us as much about who we no longer are as about who we have not yet become. Every individual's sensorial landscape is struck by this kind of degradation, which is equivalent to the destruction afflicting our forests, rivers, and shores.

But what else could we expect of a time whose aesthetic plan is commingled with a pleonasm that is doomed to reproduce itself until it no longer resembles itself? This is especially true when the resulting proliferation of hybrids illustrates the sole mode of representation of a time that, incapable of rejecting it, is condemned to an infinite restoration-reproduction-re-creation of its bodies and ideas.

24

THE VIRTUAL OR DUPLICATED WORLD

Of course, when confronted with such a grim picture, many will raise objection to the *virtual,* its "virtues" and its "vertigoes." Proponents of the virtual will also remind us that the word derives from the Latin *virtus,* meaning "strength," "energy," or "the vital impulse." "*Virtus* acts fundamentally. It is simultaneously the initial cause *by virtue* of which the effect exists and the reason why the cause remains *virtually* present in the effect. Thus the virtual is neither unreal nor potential. The virtual is within the order of reality."[1]

For this reason, it is high time we realize that there is nothing separating the reality overload from the virtual. Novalis can help us here with this observation: "We usually understand the artistic better than the natural. There is more spirit, but less talent, in the simple than in the complicated."[2] This statement may help to explain the stupefying facility with which, in barely ten years, the virtual has gradually taken the place of the imaginary—or at least how, in such a short while, we have been convinced that the modernity of the virtual can replace an imagination that has grown obsolete. The virtual is not at all the negation of reality, as everything prompts us to believe, but corresponds instead to the victory of the reality overload that endlessly overflows the real to win by objectifying the space of what does not exist on a daily basis.

In other words, parallel to the current promotion of a culture that is leading to the destruction of culture, the emergence of the virtual is slowly but surely leading us to the destruction of the imaginary.

A strange kind of violence has been working to reach this point. This violence is comparable in its results to the brutality employed—one substitution after another—by concrete dematerialization, which affects all appearances today, and the characteristic feature of this violence is that it never shows itself in broad daylight. It achieves its goals in the depths of our sensibility, taking over the obscure theater where, just a short time ago, perception and representation confronted each other.

Though the devotees of the virtual world take pains to refrain from saying what kind of tangible expropriation accompanies access to cyberspace, some cannot hide the danger of perversion that threatens "our relationship to our own bodies":

> . . . [The] profound hybridization of the real human body, the one in which we have lived since the time before our birth—with abstract but tangible formalism, with arbitrary scales of time and curvatures of space—in all likelihood will lead us to a certain misappropriation of our most integrated habits. Fundamental elements of our relationships with other people, such as the notion of "presence," are also challenged by virtual practices that defy all expectations.[3]

■

Obliteration of the body, disappearance of the other, foundering of presence: We are compelled to acknowledge that adulteration will not be long in coming, for these are precisely the factors responsible for the success of cyber sexuality. This is true even if we can also recognize the reasons for adulteration's constitutive impoverishment, which lies in extrapolating, in previously unprecedented proportions, the fear of the flesh that haunts S/M and the majority of contemporary sexual practices.

This is why, with or without a "tactile feedback glove," the new practice of computer-aided love is something more than the game almost everyone wishes to reduce it to, whether they are adversaries of the Web who have a natural interest in presenting this practice as an equivalent to pinball or the partisans of the virtual who are too concerned with the respectability of their world not to make efforts to minimize its importance.

Today, the most pronounced features of "sexual cyberculture" are quite obviously "the fuzziness upheld between male and female identity, the blend of fact and fantasy, sudden ruptures in and associations of ideas, and the uneventful transition from one role to the next, all propped up by the hyper-rapidity of communication in absence of any verbal or visual hint about the actors' real behavior."[4] Still, it is difficult not to recognize, through the fluid and reversible nature of these practices, the activity of the ideal network. Yet the price is nothing less than a transformation of desire, which will be given no rest until it submits to the flexibility required by a world in which there is no longer any point in seeking its objects, only in merging with its flows.

This is done in such a way that it is even more difficult not to be struck by the strength of the undecidability that seems to be running the game while dismantling the player. What's more, the coinciding of the medium and the message in order to strip the user of all singularity should alarm everyone, because it fulfills the wishes of the theoreticians of artificial intelligence, whose goal has always been the destruction of the unity of consciousness in order to separate intelligence, feeling, and perception.

We might simply confine ourselves to these less-than-exalting considerations if this new "undecidability" of desire, which condemns this desire to spin circles in cyberspace, did not summon up its inability to extend any imaginary perspectives within the framework of contemporary unisex eroticism.

But I do not wish to establish a cause-and-effect relationship here—

I do not know anyone capable of distinguishing cause from effect in this instance. But we should remember that the virtual is a double of reality, or, more precisely, a synthetic reality. Subsequently, once the image is involved, it is a question no longer of *representation* but of *simulation.*

Any "connectionist" would be delighted about what follows as a result of this, because "the image finally escapes from the sphere of *metaphor* to enter the world of *models* . . . [for while] the metaphor can enlighten, sometimes brilliantly, but with no real power of declension, the model reformulates an abstract content in a newly intelligible way. . . . This is the distinguishing feature of simulation."[5]

This is only a suggestion of the kind of self-caricature through which desire must pass in order to manifest within this space according to the laws of predictability and symmetry. It seems we should not be surprised if, even outside cyberspace, we see desire take on the same industrious if not downright submissive appearance. The reality overload is essentially hegemonic. Consequently, praise is heaped upon the charms of the illusory omnipotence that can be regarded as one of the master trumps of cyber sexuality, whatever form it takes. The cost of cyber sexuality is the expropriation of everything that gives desire its singularity—that is, nothing less than the infinity that haunts Sade's imaginary realm. "I would like the universe to cease existing when I have an erection," one of Sade's libertines declares, illuminating the confluence of nothingness and the absolute that seems to be the essence of the perpetual return to defiance of the realms of desire and the imaginary. It seems to be a given that in order to be modern, we must be content to forget this.

Although far from being in a position to extol the virtues of the imagination—others have already done so far better than I ever could—I do not believe it is a complete waste of time to recall the "insatiable thirst for the infinite" it is intended to quench. Further, when we pull out all the stops to substitute the programmed universe of the virtual—a universe that results from the will to master a halved reality and a universe whose effectiveness depends on its closing in upon itself—we might then say that it is no longer necessary to remember the impassioned power of desire without which the imagination is nothing.

Before the universal pretension of this will to mastery, we can think of Apollinaire, who was concerned only with

> *Losing*
> *But truly losing*
> *To make room for the unexpected find.*

A few naive individuals think it best to respond to this by luring us with the notion that the virtual gives us the only opportunity to reenter the image. But this starts falling on our deaf ears when they add the more explicit detail that

> the "fundamental virtue" of virtual worlds comes from having been conceived with a definite end in mind, [and] it is this end that must be realized and actualized, whether the application is industrial, spatial, medical, artistic, ludic, or philosophical. Virtual images should aid in revealing an intelligible virtual reality—an intelligibility proportionate to the end pursued, whether theoretical or practical, utilitarian or contemplative.[6]

This end is not one I would choose, even if "starting from the moment when the virtual worlds are developed en masse, they will with the same stroke make themselves part of our social environment, thus making themselves in their way a part of our reality."[7] Why should we take any interest in this "simulated society" with which we should concern ourselves "if only to define the notion of the property or value of a virtual instance"?[8]

■

We dare not believe in the miracle of trackability.* Everything, however, is clarified with this promise to define the property of the virtual: There is no value in duplicating this world and its meanness in order to replace the imagination.

Even if it means passing for a "network killer," which I pride myself on being, how can anyone thus encircled by the reality overload not think that the first priority is to take every opportunity to flush out its principle of redundancy, which is intended to prevail over everything that lives freely?

Once again, we can note how deeply the questions of representation and reproduction are connected. As supporting evidence, I offer René Riesel's viewpoint, that

> the seed sterilization technique known as "Terminator" constitutes the *greatest triumph of a planned economic policy: fabricating a sterile living organism*. . . . For this objective to be achieved in the plant domain, it first had to be tested, if not yet perfected, on everything concerning the not strictly biological aspect ("living" in every non-scientific sense of the term) of people's lives.[9]

*[*Trackability* is a neologism coined by the Internet pioneer Fergal Butler to describe the ability to track what has been done and who did it on computer networks. —*Trans.*]

25

CULTURAL AND BIOLOGICAL STERILIZATION

This "sterile living organism" that Riesel refers to is something we have encountered everywhere. It is what populates the reality overload. It could be the archetype of what alone has the right to be cited and claim positivism in a world where the appearance of life is used to dress up the work of death.

This organism is a major adulteration against which not much can stand—and all the more so when what would have made it possible to oppose it has become a pretext for the vile cultural parade whose multiple fanfares give rhythm to so many forms of conditioning. That these fanfares are experienced as the most splendid parties indicates only that the mutation is well on its way to completion.

Nevertheless, the innovation of biological sterilization cannot be considered "as just another ordinary merchandise intended solely as a source of more profit for the 'multinationals' and only invading *the markets*,"[1] for, as René Riesel emphasizes, the enterprise of eradicating the negative through the intervention of culture, although it borrows the methods of economics, cannot be reduced to a new example of simple "merchandising."

In both cases, a serious attack against life is under way. Biological sterilization has its counterpart in cultural sterilization.

■

For those looking for a way to picture the method of transformation of a world increasingly besieged by the "sterile living organism," the universal sacralization of sports, in spite of all the dealings with dirty money that enable them to operate, provides a significant illustration. The rationality of inconsistency already rules as master of the masses penned up in stadiums by the police and multiplied infinitely on television screens, ready to slaughter each other over a conflict that is as fictitious as it is repetitious. Such conflicts take place in confined, packed-to-overflowing spaces, where all the sordidness of the world is concentrated under the wretched guise of good intentions.

This guise is the only metaphor for a time without metaphor in which the reality overload has no goal other than its proliferating muscle-building. Even if we wanted to ignore it, refusing to open the newspaper, listen to the radio, or watch television, it is now impossible to do so. It has transformed our cities and towns into something where the gesticulations and shouts of fans force us to reckon with what is now much more than just a spectacle.

The unanimous acknowledgment of the spectacle makes it the new ritual through which the reality overload celebrates its foundations: the strength of the exalted number of the competition to the infinite redundancy of a mass whose sole purpose is to swarm; the normalization of difference with the production of its battery-reared heroes manufactured to yield; and finally, the systematic lie as the basis of an ideology of consensus serving to disguise shameless chauvinism, financial misconduct, and endemic criminality.

In fact, blissfully happy before "these athletes who *inspire dreams,*" the media hail them as a "success in the art of creating the human purebred" that the ignoble baron de Coubertin* wished to propagate. They are right, too: These are the real heroes of our time. Their bodies stripped of all erotic qualities testify only to the "docile passion" inculcated in them by their "trainer-tamers" in the manner foreseen thirty-five years

*[Pierre de Frédy, baron of Coubertin (1863–1937), was a French educator and historian and a founder of the International Olympic Committee. —*Trans.*]

ago by Radovan Ivsic.[2] Further, it is not simply their recourse to both performance-enhancing drugs and modified foods that makes them the most polished embodiment of the sterile living organism.

It would be a great mistake to place these athletes at the antipodes of the great cultural threshing. They are its complement, if not its model. Just as their bodies have been violated to turn them into organisms programmed for repetition, our minds have been assaulted to bring about the same kind of submission to a world in which the human body, like ideas, is condemned to insignificance.

It is necessary to see this assault and victory as the disastrous triumph of the celibate thought that rules us. It is an efficient thought with eyes only for itself—a manipulative thought that claims to guard against everything it is not, a strategic thought whose only objective is to improve its solitude in order to prevent any passion-sparked blaze.

On May 17, 1914, Freud wrote to Ernest Jones: "Whoever allows humanity to free itself from humiliating sexual enslavement, whatever stupidities he utters, will be considered a hero." This hero has not appeared, but our entire society has taken on the splendid project of a widespread elimination of the erotic, offering myriad substitutes for desire. This is likely one of the principal reasons for the happiness the majority place in their servitude, as well as the morality that restricts them a little more each day.

Those rare few who flee it instinctively are the only ones who oppose this happiness in submission, which is well on its way to imposing itself as an art of living. By virtue of their ferocious refusal to grant the slightest bit of significance to an increasingly suffocating and grotesque world, it is perhaps not yet entirely impossible to breathe. There are even some words, ideas, and places that this celibate thought has not succeeded in neutralizing completely. It is up to each of us to repossess them savagely. This is the new "individual recovery" that awaits those who remember the Night Workers. If anything can begin again—which is not necessarily likely—it is only through this sabotage inspired by the passions.

Meanwhile, let no one ask me to acknowledge anything in this world. Here, I am looking only for traces of life that have not been tamed. There are others who still share this passion. As for those who do not possess it—and as for whatever these people claim to represent—it is through every means possible that I intend to tell them no, no, no, no, no, no, no.

APPENDIX

THE THEORY OVERLOAD

This talk was given on November 9, 2006, at the request of Pier Buvik, director of the Center for Franco-Norwegian Cooperation in the Social and Human Sciences, during a series of conferences entitled "French Theory Revisited" at the House of the Human Sciences in Paris.

My choice as title for my intercession here, "The Theory Overload," which I deliver six years after publication of a fierce criticism of our time entitled *The Reality Overload,*[1] is due not to a lack of imagination, as some spiteful individuals might wish to believe. I think rather it is a consequence of our time—I even wonder if lack of imagination might not form the deep connection between the *theory overload* that appeared during the seventies and the *reality overload* that became increasingly visible around 2000.

At the very least, I view this as the reason why I have quite naturally kept my distance from the various philosophies grouped together under the label "French Theory." To give an idea of just how far I was from this conceptual activity at the moment when the body of theory concerning us here today first began to take shape, I quote several phrases from what I was writing then. This was in 1969.

> I have nothing to say and, even less, *something to say;* for the moment I am talking while others are dancing, yelling, sneezing, losing

> weight, killing, breathing, stretching out. . . . No one has ever left anywhere, even at the end of a sentence, without wearing a disguise. I disdainfully confess to wearing false eyelashes and to having no hammer, a minor inconvenience, when one's gaze does all it can to lose itself in the distance.

We are late, but wouldn't this only be a rain check? Day has not yet finished advancing backwards on night's belly. . . .

Rumor has it that we are traveling, but we are not running. We are suffocating under teddy-bear skins; at the end of a string, we are pulling caravans of precious, jolting, ordinary, anachronistic, useless, worn-out, marvelous—yes, marvelous—ideas. But who is speaking?

I hear nothing but the murmur of despair in beings and things at not being able to travel. As a garment skin is too tight to allow for long trips, it is the fixed source for all mistaken notions about personality.[2]

This should be ample evidence to show that I was somewhere else, and in search of something entirely different. Although at times I later tackled the same subjects tackled by Deleuze, Foucault, Barthes—whether such subjects were Sade, feminism, Creolity, Raymond Roussel, or Georges Bataille—I never referred to any of these theoreticians unless it was to state my disagreement with their views. It was undoubtedly the knowledge of this instinctive divergence that led to my invitation to speak here—especially because I do not participate in any way in the philosophical middle class that, under the pretext of a return to Kant, has sought to destroy everything that was authentically libertarian in the intellectual tumult that gave birth to the events of May 1968.

To the contrary, I am one of the rare individuals who, having taken part in this movement, have not shown themselves unworthy of it. I have never sought to exercise any kind of authority, even academic authority. Simply put, I have not denied any part of the revolt that was mine during those years. The follow-up to my various interventions over some thirty years shows that, while I have kept my distance from "French Theory" and its many forms of fallout, I have not conceded in any way to the various reactions that have asserted themselves, in contrast to some other individuals, who, with the approach of advancing age, are now opposing the modernity they once promoted, such as Jean Clair in his praise of "true" painting and Tzvetan Todorov, now concerned with the defense of "true" literature. In fact, from the return of figurative representation in art to the return of the motif, which are among the surest avenues for returning to the good old subject,* all that is truly involved is individuals repositioning themselves on the chessboard of the same cultural decorum. I have always flattered myself for not knowing the rules of this game. Further, it is the same lack of interest in these kinds of games that has led me from the onset to stay on my guard against something that, before becoming French Theory, first imposed itself as the latest in cultural chic. For the first time, theory suggested it held the possibility of countless role games for fans of verbal subversion.

It is high time that we analyze this famous theory by starting with the principles that ensured its success. I would therefore like to transform myself into a deconstructionist for a moment in order to single out the common feature shared by this mass of disparate thoughts (which are often highly incompatible with each other)—a feature that is hopelessly academic. More important, French Theory was the creation of a generation of professors, for the most part graduates of the most prestigious universities, who were impatient to exercise real power far beyond the borders of the university. For one and all of these academics, what this has involved since the beginning is nothing less than the reevaluation of all intellectual or artistic production—a reevaluation based on their wisdom.

This French Theory first asserted itself like a combination of power arrangements that are scarcely any different from those that its representatives claim to denounce. Yet its superiority over the habitual forms of power is inherent in its ability to present itself opposed to these standard power arrangements. Rather, it appears wearing the mask of a criti-

*[This is the subject that has been made to disappear by the efforts of deconstructionists and other French theoreticians. —*Trans.*]

cism of criticism that is equally indefinable and intransitive, and thus ungraspable. As spelled out by Paul de Man, "the main theoretical interest of literary theory consists in the impossibility of its definition."[3]

Indeed, by initially claiming to focus its interrogations upon itself—on its discourse and the conditions of its production—this theory succeeded in spilling over the boundaries of the philosophical realm until it managed to ensure the disappearance of literature as a distinct category and eventually annexed the field of human sciences to the literary one before absorbing all the multiple branches of knowledge.

Thus it is not by chance that the term *theory* quickly prevailed in characterizing this activity. If this term was preferred to the term *philosophy* or *thought,* it is, because of its abstract nature, that the very notion of theory suggests an intimidating construction of a nature that excludes from its inception anyone who possesses neither its vocabulary nor its rhetoric. In other words, it excludes anyone who does not immediately pay allegiance to an intellectual functioning whose trump lies in preventing any possible doubt concerning it by short-circuiting this doubt in advance.

It achieves this by claiming to be "beyond conclusion." The effect of this leads not to the avoidance of making a decision, but, rather, to the ability to claim both one thing and its opposite under the pretext that "nothing is certain," as Jacques Derrida has said repeatedly. Hence the vague nature of the concepts used to prop up this theory: from power to the difference, from writing to the will to learn, from identity to genre . . . . But what does it matter when the strength of French Theory lies, first and foremost, in its ability to make any kind of reading grid operational, provided such a grid permits its user to attain a position of mastery?

In fact, we are not very far from what, on the other side of the looking glass, Alice and Humpty Dumpty sought to define more precisely:

> "When *I* use a word," Humpty Dumpty said in rather a scornful tone, "it means just what I choose it to mean—neither more nor less."

"The question is," said Alice, "whether you *can* make words mean so many different things."

"The question is," said Humpty Dumpty, "which is to be master—that's all."

Simply because this dialogue was quoted quite judiciously by Barbara Cassin[4] at the beginning of her essay on the sophistic effect, nothing is changed. The sad thing is not that French Theory fits into this sophistic tradition, according to which the individual is only an effect of speech, but that the speech in question has been endowed with the powers of standardization through the exercise of power.

The proof for this is today's extreme rarity of essays and critical texts unencumbered by multiple references to this French Theory. Of course, we can mention the effect of style: Many of those who claim to take their inspiration from deconstructionism are the same who took their marching orders from existentialism in the 1950s. Yet this lack is also the result of a formidable ascendancy that is all the easier to accept because it requires only comprehension of its principle in order to use it to benefit on all occasions. This is something that the thriving descendants of French Theory have not yet finished illustrating. In fact, it is difficult to overlook the fact that the global dissemination of this French Theory is "inextricably linked to the unquestionable American domination of cultural industries and academic and publishing institutions,"[5] which François Cusset aptly notes, although he looks favorably upon this trend of thought. We can also measure in passing how this hope of mastery, promised to all users of French Theory, has given the advantage for some thirty years to a dreadful intellectual conformity, even though this conformity camouflages itself with ever new fields of application. I would even go so far as to describe it as intellectual servitude whose repetitious effects are not foreign to the desertification that today threatens the mental landscape.

But I will revisit this point after I've given several specific examples of the strength of the exploitation, truly the manipulative energy responsible for the success of French Theory.

I will start with Sade, specifically when Foucault declares in *The Order of Things,* in the chapter concerning "The Limits of Representation," that "*Juliette* is the last of the Classical narratives,"[6] because "Sade's scenes and reasoning recapture all the fresh violence of desire in a deployment of a representation that is transparent and without flaw."[7] But he offers this only after explaining (several pages before) that Juliette's desires "are carried over, without any residuum, into the representation that provides them with a reasonable foundation in *discourse* and transforms them spontaneously into *scenes.*"[8]

What is this supposed to mean? It amounts to nothing, unless Michel Foucault, concerned with the deployment of his fresco of the classical age into a gigantic *conceptorama,* cannot see or does not wish to see the importance of not what is ending with Sade, but what is beginning. This corresponds to the invention of a new mental space, where, for the first time, philosophy finds itself placed in the boudoir. That this takes place due to an endless bidding war between the body and the head characterizes Sade's "way of thinking." This way of thinking runs counter to not only everything in play during the classical age, but also everything Foucault is trying to convince us to believe it was. In his way of thinking, Sade shows us not only virtue offended, but also "philosophy offended," to borrow Lichtenberg's expression. This is undoubtedly the very quality Foucault cannot accept. As a consequence, he puts forth the notion, in *Madness and Civilization,* that "Sade's calm, patient language also gathers up the final words of unreason and gives them, for the future, a meaning that is more remote."[9] Thus, here the final classical narrative is transformed into "the final expression of unreason." "Here," Foucault continues, "is the source of Sade's great monotony: As he advances, the settings dissolve, the surprises, the incidents, the pathetic or dramatic links of the scenes vanish,"[10] until they attain in *Juliette* a sovereign game "whose perception is such that its novelty can be only similarity to itself."[11]

Again, just what is this supposed to mean? If there is a novelty in *Juliette,* it resides in the dramatic tension that gives this figure her incandescent beauty, which comes not only from her natural excessiveness, but even more from her role as a stand-in for nature in every sense of the word—which is to say, she betrays nature by surpassing it and surpasses it by betraying it.

As far as is possible from this "similarity to itself," Juliette is in quest of a physical awareness of the infinite, something Michel Foucault misses completely in order to develop his theory of an emergence "from the nothingness of unreason" at the end of the classical age. He goes through all this rigmarole only to inform us, finally, that Sade "bores us; he is a disciplinarian, a sergeant of sex, an accountant of asses and their equivalents."[12]

Michel Foucault also indulges himself in the reading of Raymond Roussel, but I will spare you the accumulation of misinterpretations that led him to see, for example, in *New Impressions of Africa,* "a festival" animated by "the rapid dancing of a language leaping from one thing to another, bringing them face-to-face, and from their incompatibility setting off short circuits, firecrackers, and sparks."[13] This book is actually the darkest kind of treatise on fairly ponderous matters, one in which Raymond Roussel enables us, a short time before his death, to witness the suicidal ascent of matter into language.

I will also spare you the examples of textual or aestheticizing incomprehension that Roland Barthes has displayed concerning Sade, with an obstinacy of a nature to satisfy all the gullible marks of literature, who are consequently only too happy to see simply a universe of discourse in which "the center, weight, and meaning are dismissed"[14] before going on to learn that "language—the performance of a language system—is neither reactionary nor progressive; it is quite simply fascist."[15] But it would be too fastidious a task to pick out all the errors in how representatives of French Theory have utilized literary or artistic references to develop or illustrate what they profess.

We can recall the two scientists, Alan Sokal and Jean Bricmont,[16] who flushed out the misunderstanding and nonsensical usage of terms that served as scientific reference to the majority of these representatives. It is significant that no one was in a position to contest their charges, but it is even more significant that these representatives refrained from even acknowledging these charges. Indeed, Julia Kristeva, the well-known songster of cosmopolitanism, based her counterargument on emphasizing the fact that these attacks were made by two foreigners. She even had the indecency to claim that "through her," an insult had been made "against the whole of France."[17]

When taking into consideration the great theoretical constructions we owe to these thinkers, it might be said that these criticisms are mere details. In response, I could just as easily emphasize the necessity of questioning the solidity and pertinence of great constructions that need to be propped up so often by references that are rickety, to say the least. What's more, this line of questioning appears even more justified when we consider the plethora of descendants of French Theory—and the sources and references from them that become pretexts for every kind of fantasy. I am thinking specifically of feminist deconstruction as well as the thought that presided over the formation of Creolitarian ideology, which I recently criticized for how its proponents' discourse appears to reproduce, under the pretext of liberation, the defects of totalitarian thinking.

Edward Said, speaking as an exiled Palestinian intellectual, enthusiastically remembered his discovery of French Theory in these terms: "How liberating to encounter the daring epistemological sweep."[18] Yet it is noteworthy that the theoretical terrorism engendered by this liberation, evidence for which is still provided by *Cultural Studies,* despite its claims of scientific objectivity, hardly differs from the worst Marxist-Leninist or Jdanovian interpretations in which the working class held the role now assumed by women, the excolonized, the half-caste, or the Black. What is novel here is the possibility for an unlimited number of postulants to exercise this theoretical terror.

In this regard, in 2000, when I analyzed the reality overload in which the world of merchandise drowns us, I showed how deconstructionism plays an active role through the rationality of inconsistency that it installs. In this role, it justifies any ethnic or shared identity group to impose itself as a system of exclusion that nonetheless has assimilation in its sights. In other words, what we are dealing with here is the oxymoron of an *integrated difference,* a contradiction that is not a contradiction: This is the distinguishing feature of these theoretical montages, and it inaugurates the time of what I have called the relative absolutes. Due to these absolutes, there is no longer any difference today, relative as it might be, that cannot be claimed as the unique key to the world. We owe this theoretical miracle in large part to French Theory. In fact, there can be no doubt that this theory presided over the monstrous engendering of a feminine writing in which the belly of women and what flows out of it are presented as the inexhaustible source.

It is in fact Hélène Cixous, one of the prophetesses of French Theory, who, during the 1970s, carried this "coming to writing" to the heights of the textually ridiculous by assuring us that women "live in direct contact with writing with no go-between. The song is inside me but it is a song that, once uttered, accedes to language: a flow that is immediately text."[19] Unfortunately, Hélène Cixous had emulators. Thus we owe Luce Irigaray, speculum in hand,[20] for having renewed the theoretical arsenal of French Theory by feminizing it, and for informing us, among other things, of the macho nature of the theory of fluids, but all the while placing her hopes in the fact that "the/a woman can never be contained/be shut up in a volume."

We should not be surprised that after some thirty years, this kind of textual menstrual flow has begun to dry up. Educated in the school of deconstructionism, however, the neofeminists have not been caught off guard in the slightest. They regrouped so thoroughly that when I republished a new edition of the criticism I wrote in 1977 in *Lâchez Tout* [Drop Everything] thirteen years later, I was compelled to add a preface entitled "Turn skirt"[21] in order to show how far they had come, with the help of deconstructionism, in claiming the opposite of what they had asserted loud and clear a dozen years earlier. Once again, Julia Kristeva revealed herself to be a veritable virtuosa of denial. Dazzled in 1974 by the freedom enjoyed by women in Mao's China, she wondered at that time "if the ideal of the socialist ego was not expressly designed for women."[22] In 1979, we find her suddenly dreading that "feminine revolt has become stuck in a secular religiosity without differences and without ethics."[23] In any event, the fact that human rights had been sneered at constantly in this land of women's liberty was an entirely relative piece of information that deconstructionism was able to reduce to a mere detail.

Likewise, around 1990, I discovered the subtleties employed by the feminist deconstruction of art history that led to the disqualification of Degas, Toulouse-Lautrec, Manet, de Kooning, and Picasso . . . because each and every one of them "implicitly assault[s] female reality and autonomy."[24] This is but one example of a thousand affirming the difference that leads to interpretations of the world that prevent not only comprehending it, but also changing it. In fact, it should be no surprise that the key positions in universities are increasingly awarded to the spokespeople of this kind of obscurantism. This fallacious recognition of difference turns out to be a formidable means of depoliticization.

I know that since that time, Queer Theory has entered the scene.* Starting from a challenge by the gay communitarianism of the 1980s, it appeared by the start of the following decade, just like the feminist new wave, and presented itself as a deconstructive critique of all the essentialisms—the normalizing, identity-based determinations that had the reductive effects of a binary sexualization—through the academic works of Eve Kosofsky Sedgwick, Judith Butler, and Monique Wittig. But laudable as the efforts of Judith Butler, for example, may be, in order to escape from the identity trap and cast confusion on the order of genres, which could be only a social or psychological construction, it

***Queer* originally meant "twisted" or "askew," both of which could also be translated as "strange," "funny," "shady," "eccentric" . . . and, by that token, "transvestite" or "homosexual."

is disconcerting that she finds illustrations for what she professes in the work of Cindy Sherman. In Sherman's creations we find the most derisory gender reversals pitiably reflecting nothing but themselves for more than twenty years. What's more, her work shamelessly and crudely plagiarizes Hans Bellmer, Max Ernst, and Claude Cahun . . . and all this takes place at the instigation of institutions such as museums and universities. In order to promote the subversion they hold tightly leashed, these powerful authorities have no difficulty swallowing huge sums of money. Perhaps this is "to queerize the dominant heteronormativity," which they claim to be their intention.

Thus, when Judith Butler wonders if "the denaturalization of sexual identity cannot have the effect of consolidating hegemonic norms,"[25] we cannot ignore the extent to which the reversibility of the difference—asserting itself through transvestitism as the liberating challenge of sexual identity—seems to conform to the "merchandizing of the difference (the most significant feature of *The New Spirit of Capitalism* by Luc Boltanski and Ève Capiello).[26] Their analysis of the new cultural products—products that have been generated by the notion of difference—shows that their distinguishing characteristics are threatened by the contradiction inherent in their origin. This origin consists of reproducing their singularity for mercantile purposes. Their analysis could just as easily apply to the ceaselessly recurring manifestations of Queer Theory during the course of its conceptual flight forward with which its history has become confused, subject, like the consumption of these same products, to "rapid cycles of infatuation and disappointment." This observation raises many questions concerning French Theory in its entirety. We may wonder if one of its advance duties is to provide to a world order in the process of establishing itself the theoretical instruments that this world order needs to attain hegemony. In other words, perhaps these instruments are contained in the famous "toolbox" about which Gilles Deleuze spoke in description of his concepts.

Would this be an irony of history or an irony of theory? It is too easy to blame the phenomenon of recuperation for the growing appropriateness of the hypotheses of French Theory for the new shapes taken by domination.

This was a question I raised as early as 1988 in my essay *Appel d'air* [A Breath of Air/Air Intake],[27] when I sought to learn to what extent Structuralists and deconstructionists alike, by virtue of asserting the death of the subject, the disappearance of meaning, and the erasure of history *outside all tangible consideration,* had served the technocratic society they pride themselves on fighting. Today, it appears highly probable that their hypotheses have helped to sharpen the silhouette of the "one-dimensional man" that Herbert Marcuse noted in 1964. It has even become hard to doubt this in light of the analyses of Luc Boltanski and Ève Capiello, according to whom "the redeployment of capitalism has been linked to the recuperation of the figure of the network."[28] In fact, even when they cautiously argue about recuperation, it is somewhat dizzying to see how the hypotheses of French Theory seem to be more and more in tune with the "connectionist" order that is on the verge of triumphing. Finally, how is it possible that discourses that claim to denounce the arrangements and strategies of power end up giving those powers the foundation, if not the theoretical justification, they lack?

By all evidence, the "theoretical machinations" of our philosophers have anticipated the expectations of not only the new users of the Internet, but also its promoters. Thus quite quickly, "rather than invite the *politicization* of the network and conclude that the Internet is a weapon of opposition, French Theory is first and foremost an opportunity (especially on the American side of the Atlantic) for a playful self-reflection of technique."[29] We have managed to bring about the emergence of a "recurring homology of canvas and theory, a vector of technical diffusion and a body of philosophical texts."[30] It is not merely the paradigm of the network-rhizome that French Theory shares with the "new spirit of capitalism." It is also the schizoid subject envisioned by Deleuze and Guattari in *Anti-Oedipus*—the subject who is neither man nor woman, son nor father, and who is open to every connection.

This subject is impossible to tell apart from the acritical, desymbolized, and guilt-free subject desired by neoliberalism. And what mirrors are not offered to this floating subject? With no ties, it is defined by its sexual, emotional, or intellectual indetermination so that nothing prevents it from being traversed by the tide of a generalized commodification by French Theory of yesterday and today. From the Deleuzian schizophreniac to the already delocalized subject of Judith Butler, we must also mention the "cyborg-being" of a Dona Haraway laboring on a machine future, inspired by the mechanical assemblages of Gilles Deleuze, as well as the biopolitics of Michel Foucault.

It is not Foucault's "care of the self" that finds its most connected implementation in the "self-monitoring" recommended by management to its subordinate directors. Nothing is changed by the fact that Michel Foucault committed himself to this direction after a detour through antiquity. This kind of about-face is a distinguishing feature of French Theory. Roland Barthes proclaimed, after the death of his mother, that he was no longer concerned with being modern, as if we are connected to the other when we view ourselves as theoreticians of discourse.

It is striking that French Theory has a second nature in this labile property that does not at all differ from the flexibility exalted by the "new spirit of capitalism." Though it would be easy to continue listing this way the many ways in which the numerous propositions of theoreticians and the most vivid innovations of postmodern capitalism have found common ground, I find myself still incapable of answering the question of just what French Theory could have done to oppose this convergence.

We have only to recall the kind of fascination it exercised on philosophers such as Deleuze and Guattari, thinkers who were sensitive to the vital strength of capitalism, or on Foucault, who recognized its erotic power, or on Baudrillard, who found himself in its aesthetic.

Is this a disturbing contradiction? Surely not. If in my critique of this time I've been led to bring out the notion of the rationality of inconsistency that governs, explains, and justifies most current behavior, it seems difficult to me not to view it as a consequence of the "undecidability" promoted to the rank of a capital virtue by deconstructionists. In reality, it is indifference that rules over the kingdom of difference; there is no longer any concern here with distinguishing between true and false or between liberty and irresponsibility. First of all, this is a tangible indifference. But it is also the indifference of teachers and the well-to-do who are able to treat themselves to the luxury of inconsequence. In this regard, it would be cruel to draw up a list of the successive mistakes and turnabouts that the representatives of French Theory have provided. Yet we can recall that after the 1984 discovery of the anti-Semitic and pro-Hitlerian past of Paul de Man, deconstructionism aided Jacques Derrida in his absolution of this key figure of French Theory, under the pretext that all of us are condemned to remain within the illusion of language, and that if we wish to escape this illusion, the sole solution is to bury ourselves even deeper in it.

Under these conditions, we cannot be surprised by the chronic depoliticization that in the final analysis is inherent in French Theory, despite the spectacular positions taken by some of its representatives. These are meticulous positions that, as the work of those who have found shelter in academic institutions, will greatly encourage their critical blindness. In fact, everything has transpired as if these thinkers had not seen what was coming. In this sense, Dany-Robert Dufour is absolutely correct to note, for example, that Michel Foucault, "studying the various ways in which power takes control of life, did not see that an entirely new form of domination was gradually replacing them—a form that aimed at weakening all the institutions and authorities still capable of inserting their values between individuals and commodities."[31] In other words, domination no longer tends to go through direct repression, but instead seeks to incite a tolerance that is increasingly necessary for the circulation of merchandise.

With regard to the conquest of intellectual, cultural, and artistic space, which is essential for the infinite extension of this domination, adorning itself with the colors of freedom, not only was French Theory completely taken in, but also, willingly or not, it played a major role in this conquest.

This is the greatest charge that can be lodged against French Theory, and one that targets equally its founders and their descendants. I view this as one of the most upsetting undertakings waged against emotional and imaginal life. It was during the course of this undertaking that resentment felt by the proponents of French Theory toward all who have escaped it reached its height. It started perhaps even unintentionally from the moment French Theory became a constant presence, lending a helping hand to the various authorities who, in the final analysis, are responsible for deforesting, clearing, and charting a domain that had depended until this time upon our intimacy. This is what brought us to the sight of these French theoreticians reducing the shores of the unreal, the pockets of obscurity, and the archipelagoes of darkness in which the freedom of every individual had some chance of finding nourishment. Their fecklessness has meant that they succeeded in opening the entirety of sensory space to commodification. By this token, it seems it is high time to start worrying about the "definitive dreamer" that we have ceased to be.

It was first man's cargo of perceptions, sensations, and emotions that French Theory jettisoned in order to give substance to the idea of a man reduced to his language alone. Thus, once the death of this man had been announced by Michel Foucault, even the memory of this "definitive dreamer" had to be destroyed in order that we could witness this transformation of the imaginal realm into a surveillance grid—a grid that is the sinister work of this coalition of professors. These professors play stationmasters on a global scale so they may sort, orient, and arrange everything in a hierarchy. This is through the claim of the "undecidable" nature of things that paradoxically gives them the authority not only to interpret things in whatever way suits them but also to speak in the place of those who are not armed with their theory. At heart, what Michel Foucault has claimed to do for the voiceless of history—lunatics or criminals—French Theory has done in the artistic realm by producing a discourse instruction manual for the use of those who are panicked by the sensory world.

At the very least, the results leave us perplexed. We can consider Michel Foucault's text on the famous Magritte painting *This Is Not a Pipe* in which, page after page, thought spins its wheels, incapable of grabbing on to an object.

François Cusset, meanwhile, has rhapsodized over Gilles Deleuze's contribution on painting. You might think you were dreaming on coming across this reference to Bacon that states that "art is not a question of reproducing or inventing forms, but of capturing forces."[32] This holds us until he concludes that "no art is figurative" but that all art aims at producing a force closely related to sensation." It is fortunate that Jacques Derrida, with no beating around the bush, has alerted us: "I do not believe anything like perception exists." In this way, he manages to reinforce Charles Fourier's idea of philosophers as individuals "whose self-interest prompts them to posit as insoluble every problem they do not know how to resolve."

This kind of sensorial impotence might shed some light on the constant temptation of the various discourses French Theory employs to substitute for their literary or artistic object. It is as if the very existence of this theory, truly its bidding war dynamic, is aimed only at covering up a deficiency like this. In fact, the notable aggravation of this deficiency, which has become characteristic of our time, explains the persistence of French Theory as a particularly effective decoy to lend the appearance of novelty to an activity of systematic recycling. A spectacular example of this is the bustling activity of Avital Ronell, who wishes like so many others to be a deejay of philosophy but remains in the lap of the university.*

In fact, a will of frenzied disembodiment asserts itself behind all this activity through which, once again, French Theory heralds a world

*[Avital Ronell, a professor of German at New York University, is the author of *Stupidity* (2001) and *The Test Drive* (2005) and has translated works by Derrida. —*Trans.*]

in which ideas should be without bodies and bodies should be without ideas.

No doubt, this is the culmination of a long history—one in which Blanchot plays a considerable role, with his concept of literary space as a "spaceless space" that nonetheless closes in upon itself due to the themes of ceaseless repetition, the return to the same, and the disappearance of the author, all of which are suitable for suspending even the slightest recourse to the emotional and imaginal life.

We know the sequel: All of French Theory flows from this erasure of the individual being. It should come as no surprise, then, that we have witnessed, in the flood of desiring machines and arrangements with multiple connections, the norm of a sexuality that is based increasingly on avoidance of the other and narcissistic exacerbation. The result of this avoidance is the disappearance of the body as well as the erasure of all imaginal perspective.

Of course, an objection can be raised by citing the omnipresence of the body in the various forms of contemporary expression. This is undoubtedly true, except the body now exists only as the support medium for a certain number of functions—athletic, aesthetic, and sexual—or as the obligatory reference of an art that specifically labors to decoy our attention away from its destruction. I refer specifically to the performance pieces and installations that claim to draw their inspiration from this or that representative of French Theory, in which it is obviously the erotic, symbolic, and metaphorical powers of the concrete body, the individual body, the body of the other, the body toward the other, the body of neither the one nor the other, the body that is unique because it is mortal, that they are striving to steal. We surely can see, then, that this body, increasingly circumscribed by its functional boundaries, and, by virtue of this circumscribing, condemned to echo itself, is emblematic of the aesthetic of the same—like the art of the pleonasm that flows from it—and is characteristic of the indigence of our time.

Now for the ideas without bodies: Their ravages can be measured in a new literature in which something like the eroticism envisioned by French Theory asserts itself and whose effect is to make bodies and sensations as indistinguishable as their authors. Whether these authors are homosexual or heterosexual, gay or lesbian, they all seem to be writing the same book in which bodies encounter each other, sexes enter each other and come, with the reader incapable of retaining anything of them except an overabundance of flowing fluids, secretions, stickiness, and discharges that unite, in their gumminess, the distressing unisex eroticism that is in the midst of transforming into convivial cloning.

It is therefore no accident that Jean-Jacques Pauvert noted, in his *Historical Anthology of Erotic Texts,*[33] how the erotic perspective began to appear crushed between 1985 and 2000. One of the most injurious effects of this—an effect inherent to this sexual neutralization—is that it causes us to lose sight of how representation is linked to desire. Here, too, French Theory has played a part: By praising the efficiency of self-referential systems, whether such systems concern words, things, or beings, there is a risk of causing the countless trajectories of desire to disappear beneath the figures of the same and, in doing so, stripping away the wealth of invention that, until recently, amorous representation brought within the reach of everyone.

Here is proof, *a contrario,* that everything hangs together and that the majority of our woes arise from being unable to accept this interdependence of people and things. Of course, French Theory is not solely to blame, but it has managed to reinforce one of the principal consequences of the rational choice made by our industrial societies, even if poetry did not fail to oppose this theory by reminding us, with its blinding flashes, what we owe to everything that we are not. Through both the countless forms of popular lyricism and the most singular expressions of poetic insurrection, sensory life has since found itself enlightened and strengthened in its intuitive approach, without which thought becomes mutilated to the point that it becomes mutilating.

Unfortunately, this mutilated and mutilating thought seems to be triumphing today as never before, and French Theory may constitute its most finished form in neglecting all expression that cannot be reduced to discourse. Globalization does exist, but this phenomenon is not reducible to the economic scarecrow brandished by the alter-globalists, whose discernment has been weakened by the exhausted ideas from the 1960s protest movement. Globalization also manifests through the theoretical hegemony on which deconstructionism has set its sights, even if it means separating us from ourselves and, even more, from the natural world, whose existence French Theory has completely forgotten.

Yet we all know the story about the beating of the butterfly's wings that will trigger a hurricane on the other side of the globe. Analogically, by playing the part for the whole, poetry, like love, sometimes has this kind of power to shake things up and to place things and beings in a charged state of awareness from top to bottom, thus opening them to what they are not. Hans Bellmer wrote in 1957: "The duration of a spark, the individual and the nonindividual have become interchangeable and the terror of the mortal limitation inside me in time and in space appears to be annulled. Nothingness ceases to exist when all that is not the man is added to the man. This is when he seems to be himself."[34]

The entire history of analogical thought gives evidence of these "instants of solution" whose critical dimension remains to be evaluated. This dimension is inseparable from the poetic necessity that, despite everything, continues to manifest through a passional consistency that French Theory has worked hard to render impossible, attempting to rid us of even its memory.

This is the passional consistency that unites us with the world while differentiating us from it absolutely. This passional consistency is therefore always singular—I emphasize this point—especially when the group now only manifests to deny individual life by diluting it in the multitude of its undifferentiated spectacles. This is absolutely why it is everyone's duty to recapture sensory life given us by this world when it is being stolen from us—by one red herring after another.

It is always from the darkest point of the horizon that the marvelous emerges—and it is always from the most deeply buried part of our singularity that our recognition of the other is produced. The essence of the marvelous—both poetic and amorous—is located precisely in its very improbability. Nothing is more in opposition to everything for which French Theory—past, present, and future—has served as a vehicle or will serve as a vehicle.

During the 1920s, Paul Valéry wrote to André Breton: "It is for you to speak, young seer of things." Who today would not be curious to see what he or she knows nothing of yet? We do not succeed in making ourselves seers by standing in the shadow of institutions or the light of styles. Take care: French Theory started as an institutional style that, for lack of encountering any tangible resistance, eventually imposed itself as a thinking kit.

"Once upon a time" is how fairy tales begin. Our sole chance today is to remind ourselves that we must begin by saying no, so that this time may finally be realized. While servitude is contagious, freedom is even more contagious.

NOTES

CHAPTER 1. THE NETWORK PRISON

1. Manuel Castells, *La Societé en réseaux* [The Networked Society] (Paris: Fayard, 1998).

CHAPTER 2. THE DEVALUATION OF DREAM

1. Manuel Castells, *La Societé en réseaux* [The Networked Society] (Paris: Fayard, 1998).
2. Ibid., 421–23.
3. Ibid., 423.

CHAPTER 3. LIGHT POLLUTION

1. [*Les déserts de l'amour,* title of a prose piece by Arthur Rimbaud (1854–1891). —*Ed.*]

CHAPTER 4. THE STERILE HORIZON

1. François Ramade, *Le Grand Massacre* [The Great Massacre] (Paris: Hachette Littératures, 1999), 172.
2. Roland Barthes, *Sade, Fourier, Loyola* (Paris: Seuil, 1971; reprint 1980), 11.
3. Barthes, *Leçon* [Lesson] (Paris: Seuil, 1978), 14.
4. François Ramade, *Le Grand Massacre,* 172.
5. Foreword to Ann Hindry, *Une Histoire matérielle* [A Material History] (Paris: Centre-Georges-Pompidou-Musée national d'art moderne, 2000).
6. "Questions à Werner Spies," collected by Geneviève Breerette, in "Beaubourg, d'un siècle à l'autre" [The Beaubourg: From One Century to the Next], *Le Monde,* special edition, December 31, 1999.
7. Ann Hindry, interview with Werner Spies in *Une Histoire matérielle.*

8. Ibid.
9. *Le Monde,* special edition, December 31, 1999.
10. Ibid.

CHAPTER 5. RECONDITIONING CULTURE

1. Ranier Rochlitz, *Subversion et subvention* [Subversion and Subsidization] (Paris: Gallimard, 1994), 19.
2. Ibid., 183.
3. Catherine Millet, *L'Art contemporaine en France* [Contemporary Art in France] (Paris: Flammarion, revised and updated edition, 1994), 280.
4. Ibid.
5. Thierry de Duve, *Essais datés I* [Dated Essays I], 1974–1986 (Paris: La Différence, 1987), 137.
6. Rochlitz, *Subversion et subvention,* 186.
7. Ibid.
8. Philippe Quéau, "Alerte: leurres virtuels" [Virtual Decoy Alert], cited in Ignacio Ramonet, *La Tyrannie de la communication* [The Tyranny of Communication] (Paris: Galilée, 1999), 101.
9. Nathalie Heïnrich, "Conflits autour de l'art" [Conflicts Surrounding Art], *Le Débat* 98 (January–February): 85.
10. Christian Ruby, "Art en public ou art public?" [Art in Public or Public Art?], *Le Débat,* no. 98 (January–February): 55–56.
11. Herbert Marcuse, *One-Dimensional Man* (Boston: Beacon Press, 1964), 65.
12. Ibid.

CHAPTER 6. A WIDESPREAD TWISTING AROUND

1. Guy Debord, *Cette mauvaise reputation . . .* [That Poor Reputation . . .] (Paris: Gallimard, 1993), 108.
2. Monette Vacquin, *Main basse sur les vivants* [Helping Yourself to Living Organisms] (Paris: Fayard, 1999), 100.
3. Ibid., 99–100.
4. Ibid., 101.
5. Ibid., 100.

CHAPTER 7. THE WORLD AS FALSE WITNESS

1. Marcuse, *One-Dimensional Man,* 84.

2. Ibid., 84–87.
3. Ibid., 87.
4. Ibid., 88.

CHAPTER 8. A LANGUAGE OF SYNTHESIS

1. Mentioned by Anne-Marie Lecoq in "Le Patrimoine dénaturé" [The Cultural Heritage Adulterated], *Revue de l'Art* 101 (1993).
2. Vacquin, *Main basse sur les vivants,* 105.
3. Marc Augé, Non-lieux, introduction à une anthropologie de la surmodernité [Non-Spaces: Introduction to an Anthropology of Super-modernity] (Paris: Seuil, 1992), 48.

CHAPTER 9. WHERE IS THE METAPHOR?

1. Julia Kristeva, "Une Désinformation," *Le Nouvel Observateur,* no. 1716 (September 25–October 1, 1997).
2. Ibid.
3. Ibid.
4. Julia Kristeva, *Histoires d'amour* [Love Stories] (Paris: Gallimard, 1983), 338.
5. Ibid., 338–39.
6. Jacques Bouveresse, *Prodiges et vertiges de l'analogie* [Wonders and Temptations of Analogy] (Paris: Raisons d'agir, 1999), 48.
7. Jean Maitron, *Histoire du mouvement anarchiste en France* [History of the Anarchist Movement in France], 2nd edition (Paris: Société universitaire d'éditions et de librairie, 1966), 449.
8. Remy de Gourmont, *L'Idéalisme* (Paris: Mercure de France, 1893), 14.
9. Ibid., 23.
10. Maitron, *Histoire du mouvement anarchiste en France,* 131.
11. Cited by Édith Thomas, *Louise Michel ou la Velléda de l'anarchie* [Velleda of Anarchy] (Paris: Gallimard, 1971), 308.

CHAPTER 10. POETIC OUTRAGEOUSNESS

1. Daniel Parrochia, *Philosophie des réseaux* [Philosophy of the Networks] (Paris: PUF, 1993), 6.
2. Pierre Lévy, *World philosophie* (Paris: Odile Jacob, 2000), 44.

CHAPTER 11. A NEW ORDER OF PROMISCUITY

1. "Conversation of March 22, 1831," in *Conversations de Goethe avec Eckermann* (Paris: Gallimard, 1988), 408.
2. Luc Boltanski and Ève Chiapello, *Le Nouvel Esprit de capitalisme* [The New Spirit of Capitalism] (Paris: Gallimard, 1999), 219.
3. *Télérama,* no. 2566, March 20–26, 1999.

CHAPTER 12. THE REJECTION OF THE NEGATIVE

1. Lévy, *World philosophie,* 82.
2. Ibid., 90.
3. Ibid., 98.
4. Ibid., 47.
5. Ibid., 47.
6. Ibid., 97.
7. Ibid., 184.
8. Ibid., 164.
9. Ibid., 217.
10. Ibid., 200.
11. Unabomber, *Manifeste: l'avenir de la société industrielle* (Monaco: Jean-Jacques Pauvert aux Éditions du Rocher, 1996). [Theodore Kaczynski's manifesto, *Industrial Society and Its Future,* first published by the *Washington Post* and the *New York Times* in 1995 . —*Ed.*]
12. Jean-Marie Apostolides, Introduction to *Manifeste: l'avenir de la société industrielle,* 30.
13. Unabomber, "Industrial Society and Its Future," The *Washington Post,* September 19, 1995.
14. *Libération,* April 9, 1996.

CHAPTER 13. VIRTUAL POSITIVITIES AND NEGATIVITIES

1. Emmanuel De Warisquiel, ed., *Le Siècle rebelle: Dictionnaire de la Contestation au Xxème Siècle* [The Rebellious Century: Dictionary of Twentieth-Century Subversion] (Paris: Larousse, 1999).
2. Ibid., 128, plate 1.
3. Ibid., 34.
4. Ramade, *Le Grand Massacre,* 135.
5. Ibid., 135.

6. Ibid., 135.
7. Ibid., 137.

CHAPTER 14. THE RATIONALITY OF INCONSISTENCY

1. Bellenger, cited in Boltanski and Chiapello, *Le Nouvel Esprit du capitalisme,* 186.
2. Boltanski and Chiapello, *Le Nouvel Esprit du capitalisme,* 185.
3. Ibid., 186.
4. *Le Monde Télévision,* March 5–6, 2000.
5. Boltanski and Chiapello, *Le Nouvel Esprit du capitalisme,* 560.
6. Ibid., 560–61.
7. Lévy, *World philosophie,* 64.
8. Élisabeth Badinter, *L'Un est l'autre* [The One Is the Other] (Paris: Odile Jacob, 1986), 341.
9. Catherine Trautmann, *La Lettre d'information,* Ministère de la Culture et de l'Information, no. 60–61 (February 11, 2000): 4.

CHAPTER 15. RELATIVE ABSOLUTES

1. Manuel Castells, *Le Pouvoir de l'identité* [The Power of Identity] (Paris: Fayard, 1999), 11.
2. Ibid., 17.
3. Griselda Pollock, *Histoire et politique: l'histoire de l'art peut-elle survivre au féminisme?* [History and Politics: Can Art History Survive Feminism?], lecture, École des Beaux-Arts, Paris, January 29, 1990.
4. Marilyn French, *The War Against Women* (New York: Simon & Schuster, 1992), 163, cited in Edward Behr, *Une Amerique qui fait peur* [An America Who Provokes Fear] (Paris: Plon, 1995), 247.
5. Léo Bersani, *Homos, repenser l'identité* (Paris: Odile Jacob, 1998), 113. Originally published in English as *Homos* (Cambridge, Mass.: Harvard University Press, 1995).
6. Ibid., 111.
7. Ibid., 137.
8. Judith Butler, *Gender Trouble, Feminism and the Subversion of Identity* (New York: Routledge, 1990), 158, cited in Bersani, *Homos, repenser l'identité,* 68.
9. Ibid., 70.
10. Ibid., 96–97.
11. Ibid., 97.

12. Annie Le Brun, *Lachez Tout* [Drop Everything] (Paris: Sagittaire, 1977).
13. Didier Éribon, *Réflexions sur la question gay* (Paris: Fayard, 1999). Available in English as *Insult and the Making of the Gay Self,* translated by Michael Lucey (Durham, N.C.: Duke University Press, Series Q, 2004).
14. Alfred Jarry, *The Ubu Plays,* translated by Simon Watson Taylor (New York: Grove Press, 1969), 110.
15. Millet, *L'Art contemporain en France,* 297.

CHAPTER 16. SUBTRACTIVE AESTHETIC

1. "La bicyclette créole ou la voiture française: Un entretien avec l'écrivain antillais Raphaël Confiant" [The Creole Bicycle or the French Car: An Interview with the Caribbean Author Raphaël Confiant], *Le Monde,* November 6, 1992.
2. Ibid.
3. Cited in Sandrine Mainaud, "Cindy Sherman, la femme cent têtes" [Cindy Sherman, the Hundred-Headed Woman], *Cimaise,* March–April 1999.
4. Hans Bellmer, *La Petite Anatomie de l'image, petite anatomie de l'inconscient physique ou l'anatomie de l'image* (Paris: Le Terrain Vague, 1957; reprinted 1978), 38. Available in English as *The Little Anatomy of the Physical Unconscious: Or, The Anatomy of the Image,* translated by Jon E. Graham (Waterbury Center, Vt.: Dominion, 2004).
5. Ibid., 43–44.
6. Boltanski and Chiapello, *Le Nouvel Esprit du capitalisme,* 533.
7. For more on this system of codification, see ibid., 539.
8. Ibid., 538.

CHAPTER 17. SENSORIAL CLIMATE CONTROL

1. *Le Monde,* January 10–11, 1999.
2. Boltanski and Chiapello, *Le Nouvel Esprit du capitalisme,* 540.
3. Ibid., 547.

CHAPTER 18. RELIGIOSITY RUNNING WILD

1. Françoise Champion, "Religieux flottant, éclectisme et syncrétisme" [Wandering Religious People: Eclecticism, and Syncretism], in *Le Fait religieux,* edited by Jean Dulumeau (Paris: Fayard, 1993), 746.
2. Cited in *L'Express,* February 4–10, 1993.
3. Ibid.

CHAPTER 19. UNISEX EROTICISM

1. Bellmer, *La Petite Anatomie de l'image,* 48–49.
2. Robert Desnos, letter to Jacques Doucet, "De l'érotisme considéré dans ses manifestations écrites et du point de vue de l'esprit moderne" [Eroticism considered in its written manifestation and from the viewpoint of the modern mind], in *Nouvelles Hébrides* (Paris: Gallimard, 1978), 505.
3. Bellmer, *La Petite Anatomie de l'image,* 38.
4. Claire Legendre, *Viande* [Meat] (Paris: Grasset, 1999), 28.
5. Marcuse, *One-Dimensional Man,* 72.
6. Ibid., 74.
7. Ibid., 72.
8. Boltanski and Chiapello, *Le Nouvel Esprit du capitalisme,* 528.
9. Marcuse, *One-Dimensional Man,* 73–74.
10. Ibid., 75.
11. Ibid., 77.
12. Ibid., 77.
13. Ibid., 78.
14. Boltanski and Chiapello, *Le Nouvel Esprit du capitalisme,* 443.
15. Ibid., 171.
16. Ibid., 173.
17. Ibid., 183.
18. Ibid., 184.
19. Desnos, "De l'Érotisme," in *Nouvelles Hébrides,* 110.
20. Catherine Breillat, *Le Livre du plaisir* [The Book of Pleasure] (Paris: Éditions No. 1, 1999), 9.
21. Ibid., 62.
22. Ibid., 163.
23. Ibid., 9.

CHAPTER 20. S/M, OR SEXUAL ROLE-PLAYING

1. Badinter, *L'Un est l'autre,* 341.
2. Ibid.
3. Cited in Bersani, *Homos,* 114–45. Original English source: *Coming to Power: Writings and Graphics on Lesbian S/M* (Boston: Alyson Publications, 1987), 31.
4. Annick Foucault, *Françoise maîtresse* [Mistress Françoise] (Paris: La Musardine, 2000), 8.

5. Michel Foucault, interview with Bob Gallagher and Alexander Wilson, *Dits et écrits,* vol. IV, 743. Cited in Bersani, *Homos,* 110.
6. Bersani, *Homos,* 113.
7. Boltanski and Chiapello, *Le Nouvel Esprit du capitalisme,* 509.
8. Bersani, *Homos,* 111.
9. Charles Péguy, *Cinq priers dans la cathédrale de Chartres* [Five Prayers in Chartres Cathedral].
10. David Le Breton, *L'Adieu au corps* [Farewell to the Body] (Paris: Métailié, 1999), 36.
11. Ibid., 14–15.
12. Badinter, *L'Un est l'autre,* 343.

CHAPTER 21. CORPOREAL ILLITERACY AND GENETICALLY MODIFIED LEARNING

1. Marie-Elizabeth Ducreux, "L'Aménageable et l'irréparable" [The Reparable and the Irreparable], *Le Débat* 105 (May–August 1999): 126.
2. Paola Zambelli, "Une Régression," *Le Débat* 105:171.
3. René Riesel, "Déclaration devant le tribunal d'Agen, à l'occasion de sa comparution avec José Bové et Francis Roux, deux de ses camarades de la Confédération paysanne, lors du premier procès du maïs trangénique, le 3 février 1998" [Declaration before the tribunal of Agen on the occasion of his appearance with José Bové and Francis Roux, two of his colleagues from the Farming Confederation, at the first trial over genetically engineered corn], in *Déclarations sur l'agriculture trangénique et ceux qui pretendent s'y opposer* [Declarations on Genetically Engineered Agriculture and Those Who Claim to Be Opposed to It] (Éditions de l'Encyclopédie des nuisances, 2000), 83.
4. Daniel Cohen, *Les Gènes de l'espoir* [The Genes of Hope] (Paris: Laffont, 1993), 100.
5. Lévy, *World philosophie,* 163.
6. Cohen, *Les Gènes de l'espoir,* 69.
7. Cited in Pierre Nora, "Retour sur les lieux du crime" [Return to the Scene of the Crime], *Le Débat* 105:120.
8. Lévy, *World philosophie,* 162.
9. Cited in Alain Finkielkraut, "La Révolution cuculturelle à l'école," *Le Monde,* May 19, 2000.
10. Jean-Marc Mandosio, *L'Effondrement de la très grande bibliothèque nationale de*

France [The Failure of the Very Large National Library of France] (Éditions de l'Encyclopédie des nuisances, 1999), 70.

11. Frédéric Morvan, "Play Time ou l'impossible rêverie" [Play Time or the Impossible Dream], *Le Débat* 105:161.

CHAPTER 22. EDUCATED VANDALISM AND BODYBUILDING

1. Edward Impey, "Le Donjon de Falaise, commentaires sur sa restauration" [The Falaise Dungeon: Commentaries on Its Restoration], *Momus,* 9–10, no. 3–4 (1997): 18.
2. Example mentioned in Claude Mignot, "Dérives monumentales," *Revue de l'art* 123, no. 1 (1999): 6.
3. The "restoration" of this chateau is analyzed in Lecoq, "Le Patrimoine dénaturé," 41–51.
4. Boltanski and Chiapello, *Le Nouvel Esprit du capitalisme,* 171.
5. *Ouest-France,* May 29, 1996, quoted in *Momus,* no. 8:12.
6. David Le Breton, *Passions du risque* [Passion's Risk] (Paris: Métailié, 2000), 73.
7. Ibid., 131.
8. Mignot, "Dérives monumentales," 5.
9. Ibid., 7.
10. Ibid., 8.

CHAPTER 23. CONCRETE DEMATERIALIZATION

1. *L'Express,* no. 2511 (August 19, 1999).
2. Mignot, "Dérives monumentales," 10.
3. Cited in Lecoq, "Le Patrimoine dénaturé," 50.
4. As is said in the prospectus cited in ibid., 48.
5. Marc Augé, *Non-lieux . . . ,* 79.

CHAPTER 24. THE VIRTUAL OR DUPLICATED WORLD

1. Philippe Quéau, *Le Virtuel* (Paris: Champ Vallon, 1993), 26.
2. Novalis, *Pollen and Fragments,* translated by Arthur Versluis (Grand Rapids, Mich.: Phanes Press, 1989), 35.
3. Philippe Quéau, *Le Virtuel,* 40.
4. Joan Ullman, cited in Bruce Benderson, *Sexe et solitude* [Sex and Solitude] (Paris: Payot, 1999), 71–72.

5. Quéau, *Le Virtuel,* 32.
6. Ibid., 28.
7. Ibid., 71–72.
8. Ibid., 73.
9. Riesel, *Déclarations sur l'agriculture trangénique et ceux qui pretendent s'y opposer,* 11.

CHAPTER 25. CULTURAL AND BIOLOGICAL STERILIZATION

1. René Riesel, *Déclarations sur l'agriculture trangénique et ceux qui pretendent s'y opposer,* 11.
2. Radovan Ivsic, "Flammes sur mesure," in *L'Écart absolu,* Catalog of the XI Surrealist Exhibition, Paris, 1965.

APPENDIX: THE THEORY OVERLOAD

1. Paris: Stock, 2000, and Paris: Gallimard, "Folio essays," 2004.
2. *Tout près, les nomads,* reprinted in *Ombre pour ombre* (Paris: Gallimard, 2004).
3. Paul de Man, *The Resistance to Theory* (Minneapolis: University of Minnesota Press, 1986), 3.
4. Barbara Cassin, *L'Effet sophistique* (Paris: Gallimard, 1995).
5. François Cusset, *French Theory* (Paris: La Découverte, 2005), 302. Translated by Jeff Fort into English as *French Theory: How Foucault, Derrida, Deleuze, & Co. Transformed the Intellectual Life of the United States,* Minneapolis: University of Minnesota Press, 2008, 288.
6. Michel Foucault, *The Order of Things* (New York: Random House, 1970), 242.
7. Ibid.
8. Ibid., 210.
9. Michel Foucault, *Madness and Civilization* (New York: Random House, 1965), 282.
10. Ibid., 284.
11. Ibid.
12. Michel Foucault, "Sade, sergent du sexe," 1975, in *Dits and écrits,* vol. 1 (Paris: Gallimard, 2001), 169.
13. Michel Foucault, *Raymond Roussel* (Paris: Gallimard, 1963), 189.
14. Roland Barthes, *Sade, Fourier, Loyola* (New York: Hill and Wang), 19.

15. Roland Barthes and Susan Sontag, *A Barthes Reader,* "Inaugural Lecture, Collège de France" (New York: Hill and Wang, 1983).
16. Alan Sokal and Jean Bricmont, *Impostures intellectualles* (Paris: Odile, 1997).
17. *Le Nouvel Observateur,* September 25–October 1, 1997, no. 1716.
18. Edward Said, cited by Cusset, *French Theory,* 77.
19. Hélène Cixous, *"Coming to Writing" and Other Essays* (Cambridge: Harvard University Press, 1992).
20. *Speculum* is the title of the book that made Luce Irigaray's name, in 1974.
21. *Vagit-prop, Lâchez tout et autres texts* (Paris: Ramsay/Jean-Jacques Pauvert, 1990).
22. Julia Kristeva, *Des Chinoises* (Paris: Éditions des Femmes, 1974).
23. Julia Kristeva, *Art Press,* no. 26.
24. Marilyn French, *The War Against Women* (New York: Simon & Schuster, 1992), 163, cited by Edward Behr, *Une Amérique qui fait peur* (Paris: Plon, 1995), 247.
25. Judith Butler, *Gender Trouble, Feminism and the Subversion of Identity* (New York: Routledge, 1989), 121–22.
26. Boltanski and Capiello, *Le Nouvel esprit du capitalisme* (Paris: Gallimard, 1999).
27. Annie Le Brun, *Appel d'air* (Paris: Plon, 1989).
28. Boltanski and Capiello, *Le Nouvel espirit du capitalisme,* 547.
29. Cusset, *French Theory,* 265.
30. Ibid.
31. Dany-Robert Dufour, *L'Art de réduire les têtes* [The Art of Shrinking Heads] (Paris: Denoël, 2003), 234.
32. Cited by Cusset, *French Theory,* 241. In addition, he does not seem to have realized that Lindner's *Boy with a Machine,* reproduced in the frontispiece of *Anti-Oedipus,* is not an installation, as he says on page 246, but simply a painting.
33. Jean-Jacques Pauvert, *Anthologie historique des lectures érotiques* (Paris: Stock/ Spengler, 1995–2000).
34. Hans Bellmer, *La Petite Anatomie du l'image, petite anatomie de l'inconscient physique ou l'anatomie de l'image* (Paris: Le Terrain Vague, 1957, new edition, 1977). Translated into English as *The Little Anatomy of Desire* (Waterbury Center: Dominion, 2000).

INDEX

BOOKS OF RELATED INTEREST

Surrealism and the Occult
Shamanism, Magic, Alchemy, and the Birth of an Artistic Movement
by Nadia Choucha

As in the Heart, So in the Earth
Reversing the Desertification of the Soul and the Soil
by Pierre Rabhi

Revolt Against the Modern World
Politics, Religion, and Social Order in the Kali Yuga
by Julius Evola

Ride the Tiger
A Survival Manual for the Aristocrats of the Soul
by Julius Evola
Translated by Joscelyn Godwin
and Constance Fontana

William Blake's Sexual Path to Spiritual Vision
by Marsha Keith Schuchard

The Spiritual Journey of Alejandro Jodorowsky
The Creator of *El Topo*
by Alejandro Jodorowsky

The Primal Force in Symbol
Understanding the Language of Higher Consciousness
by René Alleau

Meditations on the Soul
Selected Letters of Marsilio Ficino
Edited by Clement Salaman

INNER TRADITIONS • BEAR & COMPANY
P.O. Box 388
Rochester, VT 05767
1-800-246-8648
www.InnerTraditions.com

Or contact your local bookseller